PENGUIN ANANDA

SANATANA DHARMA

Kripamoya Das was raised in Cornwall, south-west England, as the son of parents in the Royal Air Force. He began practising yoga and discovered the Bhagavad Gita as a teenager, and then became a devotee of Lord Krishna. He studied in India and served his guru's mission throughout the UK, Ireland and East Africa. He is a teacher of the culture and history of Sanatana Dharma, and has travelled extensively across India for many years. He lives outside London, close to Bhaktivedanta Manor, the largest Krishna temple in Europe. He travels throughout Britain, a land where thousands are fascinated by the food, philosophy and music of India. This is his ninth book.

Kripamoya Das has an online presence on Facebook, X and YouTube, and conducts a weekly reading and discussion hour on Facebook. His website is www.kripamoya.com.

sanatana dharma

Questions and Answers on the Essence of Hinduism

KRIPAMOYA DAS

PENGUIN
ANANDA
An imprint of Penguin Random House

PENGUIN ANANDA

Penguin Ananda is an imprint of the Penguin Random House group of companies whose addresses can be found at global.penguinrandomhouse.com

Published by Penguin Random House India Pvt. Ltd
4th Floor, Capital Tower 1, MG Road,
Gurugram 122 002, Haryana, India

Penguin Random House India

First published in Penguin Ananda by Penguin Random House India 2024

10 9 8 7 6 5 4 3 2 1

The views and opinions expressed in this book are the author's own and the facts are as reported by him which have been verified to the extent possible, and the publishers are not in any way liable for the same.

ISBN 9780143468349

Typeset in Sabon LT Std by Manipal Technologies Limited, Manipal

www.penguin.co.in

This book is dedicated to His Divine Grace A.C. Bhaktivedanta Swami Prabhupada, my teacher and guide, who brought the teachings of Lord Sri Krishna out of India to the world, thereby igniting a spiritual revolution on every continent

Contents

Foreword

In the pursuit of spiritual growth, seekers often encounter a multitude of questions that can either invigorate or hinder their journey. The inability to find satisfactory answers to these inquiries can significantly impact one's enthusiasm and progress along the spiritual path. Kripamoya Das adeptly addresses this fundamental aspect by identifying common queries that arise within novice and seasoned spiritual seekers.

Through concise and contemporary elucidations, he provides a refreshing perspective on age-old dilemmas, offering clarity and insight to those navigating the spiritual terrain. By delving into the depths of these inquiries with precision and relevance, the author facilitates a deeper understanding and appreciation for the spiritual journey.

The significance of this work lies not only in its ability to provide answers but also in its capacity to ignite a renewed sense of purpose and enthusiasm within seekers. By addressing these questions comprehensively and effectively, this book serves as a beacon of guidance, propelling individuals forward on their spiritual odyssey.

This is a valuable contribution that will have a profound impact on the spiritual community. May this book serve as a guiding light for seekers as they navigate the intricacies of their spiritual path.

Gauranga Das
Director of Strategy and Communications,
Govardhan Ecovillage
February 2024
www.gaurangadas.com

Introduction

Over the last 200 years, India's wisdom has gradually travelled beyond its shores to the rest of the planet. Like a refreshing spring coming to a world wrapped in winter, people have awakened to India's wonders for the first time and have found inspiration.

Millions now practise yoga, study the ancient Vedas and sing *kirtan*[*] in all the major cities of the world. It is nothing short of a cultural revolution—a peaceful, happy and life-enhancing global revolution. You might say that the uplifting ideas and spiritual traditions of India have become one of its major exports.

Preserved in the Sanskrit language for thousands of generations, the knowledge of the Hindus has stood

* Devotional song.

the test of time. Humans tend to dispose of ideas and practices that no longer help them, and that is why entire civilizations sometimes appear and disappear, as their weak foundations prove to be their undoing.

The same is not true of *Sanatana Dharma* or 'the eternal culture'. The very word *eternal* means there is no beginning to it nor will there ever be an end. It will always be of immense value to human beings who wish to be healthy, happy and peaceful, and create a better society around them. Sanatana Dharma is the very foundation of India, its pride and joy, and its greatest wealth.

I've been very lucky to be involved in teaching others about these 'ancient but always fresh' ideas for the past fifty years. It has been a great privilege to explain the oldest of cultures to modern people and see them gain a fresh understanding. The questions and answers in this short book are fragments of actual conversations. All the questions are real, so they're not always polite! But I hope you enjoy reading it and that you may even find answers to your own questions on these pages.

1

Krishna Wisdom

For as far back as we can remember, philosophers, theologians, scientists and great thinkers have discussed and debated to understand the world more profoundly. The sages of the East were no different. In the ancient body of literature known as the Vedas, they documented a spiritual understanding of the self, the universe and the deeper purpose of life. This is 'Krishna Wisdom'—essential principles that underpin universal reality.

What is Sanatana Dharma?

These are two words in the Sanskrit language. *Sanatana* means 'permanent or everlasting'. Something that doesn't decay or disintegrate can be described as sanatana. Everything in this universe, being made of atomic particles, is in a state of flux and is slowly disintegrating. It is a world made of matter. In contrast, sanatana is opposite to the nature of this world; it is something non-material or spiritual.

The word *dharma* means the behaviour of something in its natural state. For instance, the dharma of water is to be wet, and the dharma of fire is to be hot. Put together, these two words indicate the path of life that best develops our true spiritual nature.

Is it a religion?

When we follow a particular way of life, especially one centred on enhancing our spirituality, we often use the word 'religion', meaning certain beliefs and practices that will help us grow in understanding, wisdom, peace and joy. Therefore, Sanatana Dharma can also be called 'the eternal religion'. Perhaps it is better explained as a complete way of life or a guiding set of principles based on unchanging wisdom—one that is not subject to changing opinions or fashions.

Is it originally from India?

Yes, Sanatana Dharma was the very foundation of India's intellectual and spiritual culture. Today, it remains the country's precious jewel that has been carefully preserved for thousands of years. India was once named Bharata and its cultural influence extended all the way from Persia through to Cambodia and even China. In today's Greece and Russia, archaeologists are discovering Indian artefacts dating back many centuries. Because of India's dedication to higher thought, the land has been the origin of several world religions, including Buddhism, Jainism and Sikhism. Yet, despite the many varieties of philosophical persuasion, the land of Sanatana Dharma remains the most religiously tolerant and respectful country in the world.

What is the relationship between Sanatana Dharma and Hinduism?

Hinduism is a collective term for the religions of India. At one point in history, the land to the east of the River Indus became known as Hindustan and the people as Hindus. The British then added the suffix '-ism', creating the term Hinduism. Although thc word is not found in any sacred text, the term Hinduism is now widely accepted. Hinduism is not one belief system but a family of religions with thousands of members. Just as all the branches of a large tree can be traced back to the trunk, all branches of Hinduism can be traced to the ancient texts known as the Vedas, which contain the teachings of Sanatana Dharma.

How does Hare Krishna fit into Sanatana Dharma?

The largest branch of Hinduism is known as Vaishnavism, which holds that God is sanatana, or eternal. He is an all-pure, all-good, all-pervasive supremely cognizant person, who is addressed as Vishnu, 'the all-present' or Krishna, 'the all-attractive'. When Krishna appeared in this world 5000 years ago, he had a battlefield conversation with his friend Arjuna. This conversation became known as the Bhagavad Gita or 'The Song of God'.

Krishna reappeared as a great teacher named Sri Chaitanya 500 years ago. The members of Hare Krishna follow the teachings of the Gita and the path of life taught by Chaitanya.

So is the Bhagavad Gita your main book, your Krishna Bible?

There's more than one 'Bible', actually, and they are all part of a vast library of ancient wisdom. The entire library is known as the Vedas, or 'the knowledge', and the deeper, philosophical parts are known as the

Upanishads. The word *upa-ni-shat* means 'to sit down closer'. More than 100 Upanishads contain a pithy analysis of the difference between reality and illusion, and the Vedanta Sutra summarizes and rearranges their essence into a logical sequence of arguments. The Bhagavad Gita is the record of an hour-long conversation between Krishna and His warrior friend and disciple Arjuna. It contains all the major concepts of the Upanishads in dialogue form and has been read by millions for thousands of years.

Then there's another book known as the Bhagavata Purana or Srimad Bhagavatam. It's both an ancient history book and an exposition of many different levels of reality. In 18,000 verses, it analyses matter and the quantum of consciousness known as the *atma* or inner self, and further explores the reality of an unlimited, eternal world beyond the limits of our perception. All the Vedas offer knowledge of how we can be healthy and happy in this life, and free from problems in the next.

But these are all books that were written. Who wrote them?

Many sages in deep meditation received the mantras of the Vedas through mystical transmission. They preserved the knowledge by teaching it verbally to their disciples, who then taught it to their disciples and so on. It was eventually written down in the Sanskrit language by 'the original guru', Srila Vyasa Deva, who divided the Vedas into portions to make it easy for humanity to preserve. Vyasa's disciples became the founding fathers of communities that recited the portions of the Vedas as a daily practice—their descendants all over India do it even today.

Do you have to read teachings that are so old? Can't you read modern spiritual books?

Of course we can. Writing about spirituality is not limited to ancient sages and prophets. There are many modern authors who write on spirituality. But almost all of them are drawing on ancient wisdom for their inspiration too. So why not begin with reading the spiritual classics? If people are still reading a book 5000 years after it was written, you could rightly conclude that it has passed the test of time and contains perennial wisdom. Besides, the spiritual nature and experience of it are the same today as it ever was, so there's really no such thing as 'modern spirituality', only spirituality addressed to modern needs, in modern language.

What does Hare Krishna mean?

Hare and *Krishna* (Hare is pronounced Huh-ray) are the first two words of a great mantra mentioned in the Vedas and recited by Krishna's people each day. It goes like this:

Hare Krishna Hare Krishna
Krishna Krishna Hare Hare
Hare Rama Hare Rama
Rama Rama Hare Hare

Krishna means 'all attractive' and *Hare* means 'the eternal energy'. The other word is *Rama* (rhymes with drama) which means 'supreme pleasure'. A mantra is a sound formula with the potency to uplift and enlighten those who repeat it. The word is derived from *mana* (the mind) and *trayate* (to protect and free). The ultimate reality is described in the Vedas by many names, and Hare, Krishna and Rama are three of those names. When the Americans and Europeans first saw the devotees of Krishna in the 1960s, they termed them the 'Hare Krishna Movement' or 'The Hare Krishnas', and the name stuck.

Why do you sing in public?

Because the mantra elevates the mind and allows anyone to tap into the natural, spiritual happiness that lies within them. So it's good to share. Even if someone doesn't understand the language of the mantra or its meaning, there'll be a beneficial spiritual effect. When a mantra is recited softly, it benefits only the person who's repeating it, but when the mantra is said out loud it can benefit anyone who hears it. If the mantra is sung to a melody then the recitation is known as kirtan, and when sung in a public place, the mantra singing becomes *sankirtan*. Musical kirtan is an enjoyable way to meditate—even in the middle of a busy street!

How does a mantra work?

Nowadays, the word mantra has been borrowed by journalists to describe any repetitive slogan or phrase. They sometimes talk of a politician's mantra, meaning a much-repeated claim on the campaign trail. But it's not just any word that can be a mantra. A mantra is an authentic word or phrase taken only from the Vedas. It has intrinsic spiritual power, and when employed correctly, at a time of deep meditation or prayer, will have the desired effect. The repetition of the mantra calms and quietens the mind, sets it free from unhelpful cycles of desire and aversion, and focuses it on transcendence. Through mantra meditation, we rediscover our authentic selves deep within the heart and experience an awakening to joyful inner happiness. The fact that they work can be validated by the many thousands who chant them each morning. Genuine mantras are given freely but come with a set of guidelines so that the maximum effect can be gained.

Don't you just zone out when you chant mantras so much?

Not at all. There are so many ways to 'zone out' but meditation isn't one of them. With digital technology, the opportunities for placing the mind in a semi-stupefied state have greatly increased. Virtual reality of different kinds has only resulted in a lack of clarity. The mind is made to oscillate between hankering for something in the future and lamenting for something lost in the past—very rarely are we in the present reality. As a result, many people spend hours each day in unhelpful states of mental confusion. For people on a spiritual path, the present moment is extremely important since that is substantial. Mantra meditation places you in that present moment and then transports you to a timeless state where the mind can be fully refreshed and enlivened. So actually, mantra meditation is a 'zoning in'.

Don't you lose your individuality by becoming a Hare Krishna?

That's a question we used to be asked thirty years ago, when almost all of our members lived in communities—sometimes in the same house—and wore the same clothing. The success of the movement has meant that we have multiplied in number many times over and the diversity in the lives of our membership has broadened as a consequence. These days, you would be hard-pressed to know who a devotee of Krishna is just by looking at them. Although the philosophy and theology of the movement are common to all, there is a striking variety of ethical and political opinions expressed by our members.

What are your basic teachings?

In a very small nutshell, they are as follows: The soul is spirit and the body is matter. The body is a vehicle for the soul. The body is temporary but the soul endures. The soul is never born and never dies. It is unchanging, primeval and a spiritual spark of life within the body. The soul is conscious and blissful by nature. When the soul identifies with matter, it mistakenly imagines that the body is the self. In its original state, the soul is unlimitedly happy, but when it forgets its divine nature, it struggles to achieve even temporary pleasure. The soul is looking for the happiness it once had but in the wrong place. Just as sunshine comes from the sun, souls emanate from the supreme source. That ultimate reality is known in the Vedas as Brahman, Narayana or Krishna. That Godhead is not merely an impersonal energy, but the energetic source of all existence.

The souls are infinite and dependent on the Godhead, just as the rays depend on the sun. God has attributes, such as form and beauty. God has compassion and love. All souls emanate from the Supreme Being and share His loving nature, as sparks emanating from a fire share, to a very small degree, the fire's heat and light. Some souls leave their relationship with the Supreme Being to experience life apart in the world of matter.

Over countless births, layers of psychic conditioning cover their remembrance of their original nature and the hearts of these forgetful or 'conditioned' souls grow hard. By listening to spiritual messages, such as in the Bhagavad Gita, and applying them in their lives, the hearts of those souls will once again become soft and they will return to their original home with the Supreme.

Isn't the Supreme Being you speak of more of a spiritual oneness we merge into?

A great sage once said that 'When a green bird flies into a green tree, it may look as if it has disappeared, but it remains an individual bird'. The idea of merging into a divine substance is popular. Individuality seems to come along with anxiety and pain, and things don't improve when we share our lives with others. Relationships can also be a major cause of disappointment.

So when we think of existential freedom, the idea of a divine white light seems immediately attractive. But freedom from problems isn't the highest happiness; it's merely a negation. Real spiritual positivity lies in discovering our true spiritual individuality and enjoying it, and that can be best done by experiencing the bliss of our original relationship with the Supreme.

Buddhism speaks of nirvana, the extinction of all desire and consequently the illusion of individuality. What do you say to that?

The Sanskrit term *nirvana* first appeared in the Vedic literature, which pre-date Buddhism, so its meaning was originally something slightly different. *Vana* means 'wind' as in being pushed around on a gusty day, or by waves on the sea. *Nir* means a cessation of, so *nirvana* means 'no more wind'. The word is used to describe freedom from being pushed around by the winds of selfish desire and rebirth in material existence. But it is grammatically negative and, by itself, the word does not signify a positive state beyond the 'vana'.

So in the Bhagavad Gita, where the word appears five times, it is prefaced by the word *Brahma,* a supremely positive word meaning the absolute platform of spirit. Krishna explains that *brahma-nirvana* means not an impersonal absolute but a mystical union of the soul in devotion, where both God and the individual soul retain their individuality.

2

Spirit Matters

In a world where short-lived physical enjoyment is the goal, and accumulation of material goods the means, we should expect that people are at least happy some of the time. Yet the reverse seems true—restlessness and frustration are all too common, and the world now seems unable to produce sufficient resources to support our increasingly materialistic lifestyle. Our existence as spiritual beings is an idea that needs investigation. If true, our happiness may lie just beyond the range of the senses, and meditation may just provide the means to achieve it.

What do you mean by the word 'soul'?

The word 'soul' is an English version of the Sanskrit word *atma*, which means 'the self'. The body is a complex arrangement of chemicals, none of which are conscious. The body is the unconscious, external covering of the conscious soul. The atma is the source of consciousness in the body.

Isn't the brain the source of consciousness?

The brain is an organ of soft nervous tissue contained in the skull that functions as the coordinating centre of sensation and nervous activity. However, since scientists cannot adequately explain how unconscious chemicals become conscious, they admit that consciousness, as a phenomenon, must be considered separately from the functions of the brain. That is why 'consciousness studies' have now become a distinct area of scientific research. It has been shown that consciousness has the ability to observe distinct, remote phenomena without the intermediate brain and senses. In a series of laboratory experiments, detailed drawings and designs were viewed and reproduced by the subjects at a distance of several miles from their targets. The results all pointed to a conscious observer that exists outside the brain. No one is quite sure how that works, but the phenomenon was repeatedly investigated for more than two decades.*

So you're saying that the soul is consciousness?

Consciousness is a symptom of the soul, and the soul is conscious. The soul is the life within the body and its power pervades the entire body. The soul is the ultimate level of the self and the real perceiver of the world. The soul enters a bundle of cells at conception and when it departs from the body—when the soul and the body separate—we call that death.

Does everyone have a soul?

Actually, it's the other way around—you don't have a soul. Rather, you are the soul and you have a body. You're not a human being that has spiritual experiences; you're a spiritual being that has human experiences. But to answer your question—yes, everyone is a soul within a body, including every animal and plant.

What real difference does it make if I think of myself as a soul?

If it's true, then it makes an enormous difference. Thinking of yourself as something you are not is

---

* Harold Puthoff, Edwin May and Russell Targ, 'What Do We Know About Psi? The First Decade of Remote Viewing Research and Operations at Stanford Research Institute', *Journal of Scientific Exploration* 33(4) (2019), 569–92.

unhelpful, especially in the long term. It's like turning left when you should have turned right; the farther down the road you go, the more lost you are. If your identity is spiritual, then you won't find physical pleasure fully satisfying. You'll always be looking for something more, buying more and working harder to get money to buy it. With limited resources on the planet, we could all do with less stuff and more real happiness. So thinking of yourself as a soul could immediately help you and the planet.

How would you define real happiness?

When the pleasure is material, it's temporary; it has a beginning and an end and results in frustration. Because of this, material pleasure can never lead to a sense of fulfilment. We'll always be left wanting more—and that's a shame because there's a much better way to be happy. The Bhagavad Gita says that we'll be happier enjoying a permanent pleasure that comes from deep within and doesn't depend on external things.

But I'm generally happy enough as it is. Why should I try for more?

Happiness is something we experience in different amounts, and much of what we call 'happiness' is simply the temporary relief of suffering. That's a poor form of happiness. But there's more; a happiness so great that it goes beyond any delights of this world—

an ocean of happiness compared to a puddle. Wouldn't you like to experience that? The Bhagavad Gita offers the alternative—a world beyond our perception, a world in which we can experience something called *ananda* or 'bliss'.

Okay, so how would I 'transform' my consciousness?

It begins with meditation—the gradual drawing of our consciousness away from the mundane and temporary to the transcendent and infinite. Meditation can be done at any time and in any place, but the easiest method is to begin each day with a dedicated period of meditation.

What is meditation?

Meditation means to hold one thought within the mind for a period of time; to deeply contemplate it, even to become absorbed in it to the exclusion of all other thoughts. The original yoga texts say that the mind is constantly fluctuating from thought to thought. One thought leads to another and another—a chain of thoughts. These thoughts come from sensory stimulation from our current environment, or they can come, unexpectedly, from incidents in our past lives. The total effect is like ripples in a lake. The yogis say that the bottom of the lake is where you have dropped a precious golden ring, but the constant waves of thought prevent you from seeing any deeper than the surface. Meditation stills the waves of thought and allows you to see your deeper self.

Why is it important to meditate?

Our life is a spiritual journey. That's what we're made for. It's not just about getting educated, working, having a family and then dying. So every day, we need to take a few small steps along that journey. That way, as life goes by, we'll become spiritually awakened. But our tendency is to do things that really don't help us on that journey. Our minds are always dragging us here and there, and we end up falling prey to bad habits. Meditation helps us be peaceful and bring our lower self—the mind and senses—under the control of the higher self, the soul. When that is done, we lessen the risk of committing unhelpful actions and become spiritually stronger.

Should I sit quietly and do silent meditation?

You can do that, of course. You can find a method of meditation that works for you. In an increasingly noisy world, where every bleep and ringtone is a clamour for your attention, there's great value in just switching everything off and listening to the silence. Your mind needs a break sometimes. You might even want to extend your silence over a weekend in the countryside. The sages say that the sound of birds is very good for helping the mind be peaceful.

However, you may be interested to know that the classic texts on meditation don't actually recommend silence as an active meditation. Mantras are said to give us access to the greatest silence—the transcendental platform that is illuminating, all-blissful and permanently free from noisy distractions. That's why classical meditation mostly prescribes mantras. They are not ordinary sounds and lead the mind to the greatest peace.

How does it work?

There's an old poem that says that your mind is like a mirror. You look in the mirror but it's grimy from many layers of dust, placed there by your actions over many lifetimes. You can just about see your own reflection, but only very dimly. The mantra works by gradually cleaning your mind of all that dust, enabling you to see yourself as you truly are. That's why the process is called self-realization.

3

Karma and Samsara

If each of us is a quantum of consciousness inside a steadily changing physical body, a spiritual passenger in a DNA-engineered vehicle, what exactly determines our personal rollercoaster ride along the way? The materialistic world view would have it that we are all helpless victims of some inherited biological coding and that everything else is a random coincidence. But perhaps the karma of life is simply a science waiting to be discovered.

What exactly does *karma* mean?

The word 'karma' means action. Everything we do, for any reason, is known as karma. Every action creates a reaction known as *karma-phala* or 'the result of the action'. When we experience the results of our actions, it creates further desires, which makes us act again. So there is an endless chain of action-result-desire-action. This chain of karmas and karma-phalas can either be helpful or a hindrance, depending on whether our actions are good or bad.

What would you describe as a bad action?

If our words or actions cause anxiety, pain, fear or misery to others, or if we take something that doesn't belong to us, that's a bad action. It affects our present because doing bad things to others lowers our spiritual focus, and it affects our future too, because all our actions—both bad and good—come back to us sooner or later, and we'll have to deal with the consequences. A bad action is also when we act in any other way that spoils our chances of transforming our consciousness and achieving higher, spiritual happiness.

Do you mean bad karma?

Both good actions and bad actions—good or bad karma—will come back to us in the form of karmic reactions. Good deeds come back to us as good reactions, and when that happens, we experience pleasure. Bad reactions come back to us as anxiety or pain. The long chain of good and bad reactions is known as *samsara*.

But aren't 'good' and 'bad' relative? Isn't it okay if we all just follow the laws of the country we live in?

There are variations of good and bad for sure. Driving on the left-hand side of the road is certainly a bad deed in the USA and will get you arrested, while over here, it won't. It's not a matter of opinion. Similarly, having several wives is considered a crime in Great Britain, while in other countries, it's not. But there is a universal right and wrong, good and bad, that is understood the world over. That is because the laws of karma are universal and don't always resemble man-made laws or popular opinions of what is good and bad. Like the law of gravity, these laws of karma are universally applicable.

How do we know what is bad and good karma?

They are listed everywhere in the Vedas. For instance, a short list is given by Sage Manu: perseverance (*dhriti*), forgiveness (*kshama*), self-control (*dama*), sanctity or purity (*saucam*), control of senses (*indriya-*

nigrah), reason (*dhi*), knowledge or learning (*vidya*), truthfulness (*satya*) and non-violence (*ahimsa*). Lord Shiva echoes these, and also adds the cultivation of compassion (*daya*), generosity (*dana*) and austerity (*tapasya*). Another great yogi, Patanjali Muni, adds: 'Do not covet what others have' (*aparigraha*), 'Do not steal anything' (*asteya*), 'Cultivate satisfaction with what you have' (*santosh*), 'Serve a teacher of sacred lore' (*guru-sevanam*) and 'Surrender to God' (*ishvara-pranidhan*).

In the Bhagavad Gita, Sri Krishna further explains that intense desire, greed and anger are the three gates that lead to darkness. To understand what a bad action is, you just imagine the exact opposite of any of the good actions. For instance, the opposite of forgiveness is vengeance, the opposite of self-control is self-indulgence and so on. Good deeds keep us on the path of dharma while bad deeds distract us from it.

That's a long list! Is it possible to be such a good person?

Bad actions begin with bad thoughts and feelings, and good actions begin with good thoughts and feelings. It all starts with cultivating good thoughts and avoiding the bad ones. Holding on to good thoughts throughout the day means that you have to begin the day with good thoughts. That's why people start the day with meditation. If you meditate before breakfast and before you start work, you'll have a very good chance of thinking, feeling, willing and acting good all day. Meditation can be used to control the mind just as reins are used to control horses. In the Bhagavad Gita (6.6), it is said that your mind can be either a good friend or a bad enemy. You have to 'conquer' it first, otherwise it will give you endless problems. Hence, being in control of your mind and not allowing it to wander as it tends to do, is essential.

Do you believe in more than one life?

Yes. If we have not exhausted our stock of karmic reaction before the end of one life, we take birth again and continue in another life. This is sometimes known as transmigration of the soul or reincarnation. So the soul passes through one life after another. The soul is the passenger in the body, which is the vehicle. The soul remains the same but the bodies change.

In each life, the soul passes through successive stages of birth, youth, old age, dwindling and death, and each time the soul mistakenly identifies with the body. In one life, the soul thinks: 'I am a man' or 'I'm quite rich,' and in the next 'I am a woman and a mother, and this is my husband'. In yet another, the soul thinks: 'I am a horse' and 'I quite like this grass'. The soul may go down through many species of life before coming up again to the human body. It is like being pinned to a wheel of changing bodies—a revolving door of reincarnation.

So you believe that a man can become a horse in his next life?

A soul can enter into the body of any species of life, according to the activities of his previous life. It is not that a man becomes a horse, merely that the soul temporarily inhabits the body of a horse. The soul never becomes a horse—it remains the same in every life. If the soul has performed a lot of good karma, then it may even take its next birth as a God in a heavenly region. But human life is the crossroads where you decide where you want to go—and you must choose to act accordingly.

I still don't see why I would even want to become a horse though, or anything else. Can't I just stay as me?

You're still you! In every lifetime, you're always you. You never change, and will never be anyone else apart from you. Think of it this way—you wear a suit to the office, you come home and change into something casual. You are not your clothes but the person inside. Despite having changed your appearance, you remain the same. Another example—you drive an old, cheap car and then you sell it, and buy a new and more expensive model. You were the driver of the old vehicle and now drive the new one, but you remain the same person. Similarly, you, the soul, are inside a vehicle made of flesh and blood. It lasts for some time and then you get a new one—but you always remain the same person.

Why can't I remember my last life or any life?

Sometimes it's difficult to remember what we were doing yesterday, what can I say of many years ago? The trauma of being squeezed through a birth canal has an effect on us, as do the identities provided by those around us, such as parents, siblings, relatives, teachers and other adults. Forgetfulness is relatively easy in such conditions, and our identification with our new body, and the drive to experience pleasure and avoid pain, all conspire to lock us in tight to this new physical and mental package. Sometimes, children do remember their past life, usually before the age of eight, but if the parents don't accept the reality of a previous existence, the child also rejects its memories as nothing more than a dream.

If I can't remember my previous life, what can I learn from it?

We may not always have recollections of specific incidents, but the aggregate of all previous experiences is accumulated in the form of impressions. This is known as *samskara* and creates strong tendencies in our present life. There are abilities passed from life to life, such as an aptitude for an area of knowledge or a particular physical skill. Then there are irrational fears that get transmitted due to previous life trauma. Thus, one person appears wonderfully blessed as a child prodigy while another is crippled by an unexplained phobia. So although the learning does not come in the form of individual lessons learned from recollected incidents, it comes as unconscious internalized knowledge.

How can anyone be sure there's life after death?

These days there is enough anecdotal evidence to suggest that consciousness can exist outside the brain. People are regularly reporting out-of-body experiences while under anaesthesia or at times of physical trauma. Experiments conducted at research laboratories in the USA conclusively proved that 'remote viewing'—the ability to view detailed information at a distance of many miles—is a scientific fact.* Other researchers have delved into accounts of 'past lives' from around the world. People have been sharing clear memories from their previous lives and then having those facts checked. Most of these people did not believe in reincarnation and had no religious affiliation. If

* Harold Puthoff, Edwin May and Russell Targ, 'What Do We Know About Psi? The First Decade of Remote Viewing Research and Operations at Stanford Research Institute', *Journal of Scientific Exploration* 33(4) (2019), 569–92.

consciousness can exist outside the brain, it can survive the 'death' experience.

What's at the end of the chain of lives?

Each life is like a classroom in a long learning experience. Ultimately, the soul must learn all the lessons from an almost limitless number of experiences over thousands of lifetimes. The cumulative effect of this is that the soul becomes exasperated with repeated attempts to find lasting happiness in the world of matter. Only when this material exhaustion takes place does the soul begin to explore an alternative method of achieving deep and lasting satisfaction. This gradual search for *moksha* or freedom is known as yoga. The philosophy taught by Sri Krishna in the Bhagavad Gita recommends a path of dedicating all one's actions to the Supreme Being as the most efficient means of speedily perfecting the human form of life.

Is yoga a kind of meditation or a set of postures?

The Sanskrit word 'yoga' means 'to link' and describes activities by which someone can awaken their perception of their spiritual nature and bring about gradual awareness of God in themselves. Since everyone has different inclinations and abilities, there are several kinds of yoga.

Action yoga is for the physically active, knowledge yoga is for the scholarly and meditation yoga is for the mystical. The Sanskrit terms for these are *karma-yoga, jnana-yoga* and *dhyana-yoga*. The physical postures and breathing exercises taught as yoga in many modern cities are a part of dhyana-yoga.

Which one do you practise?

In the Bhagavad Gita, the different forms of yoga are described and compared. Ultimately, Krishna sums everything up by describing a form of yoga that delivers the best results of all three. It is known as the 'most secret of all secrets' and 'the perfection of yoga', and is known as *bhakti yoga*. Bhakti means a life where the practitioner orients life so that the Absolute Truth is at the centre. A gradual awareness of one's relationship with the supreme is achieved at the same time as self-realization takes place.

The liberated soul has reawakened the original love of the soul and their journey culminates in a deep feeling of being loved in return. This perfection of yogic practice is cultivated by the different aspects of mantra meditation, pure habits, study, ritual and personal disciplines. Bhakti yoga thus means linking with God through all actions, gradually leading to an uninterrupted consciousness of Krishna, or God.

Does the soul have a form?

The soul has an eternal form and identity, and a relationship with Krishna. But in the conditioned state, the soul forgets this identity. It is said that the soul in this forgetful period is only present in a 'seed form' and as it progresses, it regains its identity. Other saints have explained that the individual soul in this forgetful stage has none of its eternal characteristics, which must be given by Krishna again in response to the devotion of the soul.

What is the soul doing in this world?

Souls possess free will, which means that they can decide to love God or turn away from Him. God never forces the souls to love Him, for to do so would nullify their free will and render the love null and void. It is a fact that the souls within this world are in a state of rebellion against God, having used their free will to reject His company. Becoming enamoured with this world, they are born again and again until they realize that their true home lies elsewhere.

What happens if you die and there's actually nothing there?

In modern Western philosophy, betting that God actually exists because it involves less risk is called

Pascal's Wager. The argument is named after the seventeenth-century French mathematician Blaise Pascal (1623–62), who said that every one of us is, in fact, betting that either God exists or that He doesn't. He urges us to bet that He does, since if we do, and He does exist, it will lead to eternal life. We will have led a good life and only have lost a little income or perhaps some personal pleasure along the way. But if we use our life in denial of Him—in effect betting that He doesn't exist—we may lose everything in the life after this one.

4

Logic of the Absolute

There is a notion that having a belief in God is intellectually immature or philosophically naïve, and that what we call religion is nothing more than the enactment of ritual and mythology. Faith in a transcendent reality is routinely challenged by those who claim that God is no longer relevant. The market has become flooded with elaborately worded and stylishly packaged books propounding the death of religion. Such propositions have entered mainstream culture without much robust challenge, heavily influencing the unassuming and trusting layman.

Spirituality, the Vedic teachers remind us, has an entirely logical and scientific basis. Whereas some spiritual paths culminate in faith, the Bhagavad Gita explains that faith is only the beginning of one's journey to Krishna. As one undertakes spiritual practices with enthusiasm, patience and determination, we can begin to directly perceive the spiritual reality. From the hypothesis we undertake the experiment, and eventually arrive at an observation and conclusion.

You mentioned Krishna or God—do I need to believe in God to do yoga?

'God' is an old English word coming from the German word *Gute*, meaning 'that which is good'. Ultimately it comes from the Sanskrit word *Huta*, which means 'to whom we offer'. Usually, in the Western world, when we say the word 'God', the image of the aged man with a white beard appears in our mind. That's an artistic image but not a concept that stands up to philosophical discussion.

God is infinite and eternal, the controller of everything, and both the transcendent and the indwelling witness within us. God is the entirety of all existence, the origin of all but one who has no other origin. There are many names of God, in all the languages of the world, but ultimately God is one.

Real religion, the process that helps us to be improved versions of ourselves, is not man-made but comes from the ultimate source. So yoga and the concept of an ultimate personal God have always been intrinsically related.

The author of the ancient yoga text, Yoga Sutra, Patanjali Muni, says emphatically that the culmination of the yoga path is *ishvara-pranidhan* or 'surrender to God'.* Yoga actually means 'union with God'.

---

* Prof. Edwin Bryant, trans., *The Yoga Sutras of Patanjali* (India: Pan Books, 2018).

But why do I ultimately need a religion? Can I not just be a good person?

Theoretically, you don't need a religion. You can be a good person without religion. But how would you know what is good and what is bad? You would have to sit with others and come to a joint decision as to what is good and bad. And this might change from one year to the next, as we often see. The result is that both good and bad become arbitrary values. It is hard to derive lasting virtues from endless discussions. The net result is that both virtue and vice become meaningless terms.

That is why most cultures derive their understanding of ethics and morals from a scripture that is either God-given or God-inspired. Even if there is no such thing as God, there is great value in religious scripture because the moral principles contained within it have endured within human society, and been proved of great value to millions of people, generation after generation. And once you agree to share common values with others and strive together to follow them, you have a religion of sorts even though you want to avoid it.

In your opinion, what should everyone be striving for?

According to the Vedas, the goals of a progressive and civilized life are to follow moral and ethical principles (dharma), to work according to one's occupational duties in order to secure everything necessary for health and happiness (*artha*), to enjoy the legitimate pleasures which flow from these (*kama*) and to move towards spiritual emancipation (moksha). The Puranas state that further than this, everything should be done in a spirit of service to God. When human beings fail to do this, life is 'simply a waste of time'.

How can we know that God exists?

You can be convinced intellectually by studying the logical arguments given to explain His existence, but these in themselves are not proof. You won't know for sure. You could be swayed by the attractive emotional features of a religious path, or be moved by the sentiments expressed by others, or the good works generated by those who say they believe in God. But you still won't know for sure. The only real way is through your direct experience. Ultimately, it is only when you have direct experience of God that you can say that you 'know'. But along the way, you can feel your progress and receive assurance from Him that you are on the right path.

But if God exists, why doesn't He just show Himself to everyone?

He is already showing Himself to you, but you need help to see Him. Don't be surprised if you can't see everything with your two eyes. For example, your brain exists but you've never seen it. You have faith that it's there, but you can't actually prove it. An MRI machine can show it to you, of course, but with your unaided eyes, you can't prove that your own brain exists. So it's more a question of your ability to see God rather than His willingness to show Himself.

It would solve the question if He showed Himself to us though, wouldn't it?

He does eventually, but we need to become qualified first. The Upanishads contain many statements reminding us that neither our physical senses nor our mundane reasoning are sufficient to see God. Verses such as these:

'His form is beyond physical sense perception. No one can see Him with material eyes.'*

'The eye does not go there, nor speech, nor mind.'†

'The Supreme Self cannot be known by any amount of discourse, intelligence or hearing. Rather, He fully reserves the right to reveal Himself to whom He chooses.'‡

So although we desire to see God, if only to prove His existence, He alone will choose the time. We can hasten that moment by becoming qualified to see Him.

* Svetashvatara Upanishad 4.20.
† Kena Upanishad 1.3.
‡ Mundaka Upanishad 3.2.3.

Why does God only show Himself to a select few?

He shows Himself to everyone. No one gets left out. God doesn't have any chosen people or favourite tribes or countries. There's no race or ethnicity that is specially blessed and no particular religion either. God is not a Christian, Jew, Muslim, Hindu, Sikh, Jain or Buddhist. He has no religion Himself but is always ready to give Himself completely to whoever is interested, no matter who they are. In the Bhagavad Gita, it is described that everyone—all souls—are on exactly the same spiritual path. The difference is in how much they choose to show themselves to God. It is not God that is not ready to show Himself, but us.

Has anyone seen God?

Of course, there are so many who have seen God. Throughout history, great persons such as Prahlada, Dhruva, Suka and Vyasa have all seen God face to face. Their careful directions reveal how they were able to have such transcendental visions, and how we can too. Such visions are not the result of sentimentality or imagination, but rather the result of philosophical discrimination, disciplined eating, sleeping, breathing, rigorous discipline of the mind and unalloyed devotional service. To see God means to take complete shelter in Him, understanding that He is your maintainer and protector. It entails doing all things that please Him and nothing that displeases Him, and dedicating your very soul to His service. This is known as *saranagati*, or the path of attaining divine grace.

Isn't religion just a psychological crutch?

If you mean to ask: 'Isn't religion just a product of the human mind and God a product of human hopefulness, an idea to help us when we feel weak?' then the answer is no. When you feel hungry, you're not imagining it; you are actually hungry. When you eat, you are not using a 'psychological crutch'—you're doing the right thing. It isn't your imagination that creates your hunger—you actually do need to eat! Similarly, when we feel hungry for spiritual nourishment, we reach out for spiritual food. It is an entirely legitimate need because spiritual nourishment is the real food for the soul.

The proof of this is that when we have it in our life, we feel our spiritual hunger disappear, we enjoy spiritual feelings and we become spiritually nourished. So although traditional religion may not be popular, people still have spiritual needs. They become 'spiritual' instead of 'religious,' and may choose to refer to themselves as 'spiritual seekers,' but they still have the same aspirations.

Can't I just be spiritual and not religious?

It is a phenomenon of our times. Over the last fifty years, we've all become quite fatigued with the systems and structures of conventional religion. We point at religion as lacking in solid scientific foundation, as being the root cause of problems between communities and as a product of a pre-modern world. We have concluded that we can now do without it, so we don't bring our children up with religious education. Even in schools, it is fading away, and attendance at places of worship is at an all-time low. But people are still drawn to spirituality. They read many books about it and take courses, go on retreats, form friendships with others and meet up regularly. Yoga is enjoying popularity like never before, and teachings such as the Bhagavad Gita are known by millions. So although people say they are not 'religion-seekers', they still have a hunger for the same thing in new forms. It is fine if you'd rather think of yourself as a 'spiritual-seeker'. Don't let the labels prevent you from moving forward.

But wait, aren't we all striving to experience our own divine nature? Aren't we all God in essence?

In quality, yes, we are; in quantity, no. We are eternal, never born and always existing; God is eternal, never born and always existing. So, we share these important spiritual qualities. But we are spiritual sparks whereas God is the great fire. The sparks radiate from the fire, not the fire from the sparks. God is completely independent, whereas our existence is dependent on His existence. A gold ring and a gold mine are the same in quality, but they are hugely different in quantity—and the ring comes from the mine!

5

Happiness and Distress

Many people decry the idea of God because of the suffering in the world. They ask why, if God is all love and compassion, should anyone have to suffer, especially the innocent? Why is there evil in the world at all, if God is all-powerful? This age-old question, known as theodicy in Christianity, receives an enlightening treatment in the Vedas. Vedic sources introduce us to the concept of justice and mercy applied over multiple lifetimes. Heaven and hell are real places, the Vedas say, but not permanent. They are both merely temporary places for the onward soul to gain limited reward and punishment, and then move on.

Does the soul go to heaven? Is heaven a real place?

Of course, but it doesn't last forever. Both heaven and hell are places where we experience the accumulated reactions from our lives and enjoy or suffer according to our stock of good or bad deeds. Having experienced this, we then take birth in this world again with a fresh opportunity to choose our activities correctly and make spiritual progress.

So if our soul doesn't finally go to heaven, where does it go?

The source of all heavenly experiences is the realm of God Himself. It is the highest heavenly place. It is known as Vaikuntha in Sanskrit, the 'place without anxiety'. Once there, we never return to this world of birth and death in any form. In the kingdom of God, there is no pain or fear; there is only an unending, blissful awareness of His presence. In that spiritual sky, we live with God and enjoy our time with Him eternally.

That sounds very nice, but what about all the suffering in this world?

The laws of nature are very stringent. When we break them, there are consequences. When we stand in the rain, we get wet and may catch a cold. When we put our hand into the tiger's cage, there's a very good chance we'll be bitten—we can't blame God for our foolish choices. In the same way, when we use our phones while driving, we break the law. If we're caught, there'll be consequences and we'll be punished. Suffering comes as the inevitable consequence of not following the laws of nature or the laws of the country. But what if we're travellers and don't know the laws of a country? In the same way, we are all travellers in a strange land. We may not know all the laws of karma, but still, there will be consequences.

We can make this world a heaven or hell just by choosing our response to it. Nothing belongs to us; it all belongs to the supreme source, the one who made it, so we can only take what we need and no more. When we take more than we need, we suffer. Suffering may be regarded as a way for us wayward souls to be corrected. We are constantly being put back on the straight and narrow by a compassionate higher power, who wants us to return to Him. We can't change what happens to us in this life, as most things are beyond our control.

What we can change, however, is how we react to it. Happiness and suffering are inevitable in this world, and our best approach to solving these problems is changing our attitude towards life. When we understand that both happiness and suffering are temporary, and focus instead on cultivating our relationship with God that brings us eternal happiness, we can rise above the problems in this world. The suffering of this world is a prompt for us to aspire to leave it. This is not our real home.

But why do children suffer when they haven't done anything wrong?

Every soul creates its own future, action by action. Sometimes, an entire life goes by with no reactions to bad deeds; that soul does many bad things, but they seem to escape any form of karmic reaction. Then, in the next life, from their very childhood, they begin to suffer. When we see their lives, we can't understand why bad things are happening to an apparently innocent child. There seems to be no apparent cause or reason for their trouble. However, our response should never be a self-righteous one of attributing blame to anyone for their suffering; that is the prerogative of a much higher order. Rather, we should be thinking compassionately: 'How can I help this person?' So the reason for someone's distress is their karma, but our response must always be dharma.

It still doesn't seem fair. My aunt was very religious but she died of cancer—why?

We can never know all the intricacies of karma, samsara and the grace of God. Nor can we know what happened to your aunt in her next life. It is sad, but true, that life is indeed short and painful at times, and the remote causes of the things that happen to us—the detailed reasons we suffer loss and pain—often remain hidden. God has infinite compassion and helps each one of us in different ways. Ultimately, He draws every soul towards Him along His own path.

If we create our own karma and are forced to enjoy and suffer, how can we stop it?

We are born with what is termed *sanchit-karma*, the aggregate of accumulated reactions to all previous deeds. The portion of that accumulation that has now manifested in our current bodily form and tendencies is known as *prarabdha-karma*. Our previous karmic reactions will gradually manifest as we pass through life, and at the same time, as we continue to act, we will generate fresh reactions. The results of previous activities appear in three concurrent stages. One is called *bija* (the seed), the second is called *kutastha* (the desire) and the third is called *phalonmukha* (about to fructify). The manifest stage is called *prarabdha* (already in action). The karmic reactions cause us to become attracted to certain activities, which then creates fresh reactions. But the fact of the matter is that this chain of action and reaction can be interrupted by the process of Bhakti yoga.

How does Bhakti yoga interrupt the chain of action and reaction?

Karma is a system of education over many lives. It continues for as long as it takes for us to reorient our focus from selfish action to selfless activity. Yoga provides us with a meditative experience, allowing us to see the difference between our mental desires and our real selves to control our thoughts and subsequent actions effectively.

Meditation and prayer also connect us immediately to God, the ultimate source of cause and effect, and create a bypass to the painful educational process. It is therefore a direct method of redirecting our future.

6

Science and Religion

Someone may ask: 'How can you prove that "God" isn't just some chemical in the brain? If the spiritual experience you speak of is real, why can't everyone have it? Why does every religion say they've found the truth, and the others haven't?' At the moment, it might seem as if religion and science have always been opposed to each other—holding entirely conflicting world views. Yet both have a common interest in achieving a deeper knowledge of life's purpose, and both want to create a better world. The Vedic conviction is that they both need each other.

Are the devotees of Krishna against science?

Not at all. In fact, many eminent scientists are also theists and find no difficulty accepting the existence of a higher reality and an ultimate source of the universe. Some of them are devotees of Krishna. Science and religion do not have to be mutually opposed as they have become in the last 200 years. Both disciplines come from a search for the truth. The only difference is that one is achieved through evidence that is observable with the senses, and the other is from an internal adjustment of consciousness that leads to revelations.

But so few people can reach that meditative state. How can one prove anything is true when so few have 'seen the light'?

So few people have directly seen the tangible evidence produced from a subatomic particle accelerator hidden inside a mountain in Switzerland, and so few can understand the mathematical theories that provide evidence of those hidden realities. But those few are highly qualified specialists in their field and we trust them. Similarly, the seers, yogis and saints are also highly qualified specialists. If we offer them the same level of trust, then we'll be able to learn from them.

Yes, but a scientist can prove something in a laboratory, and another scientist can reproduce the experiment and get the same result. What you're talking about is just belief, isn't it?

Religion has faith or trust as a preliminary foundation. But at its heart, it has to have direct experience in order to be substantial. Without that, it cannot endure. In that sense, the scientific laboratory of the spiritual researcher is his own body and mind. If we make a beginning of the practice of yoga—if we begin our experiment—we'll quickly find that there is a direct, tangible experience that is observable. That experience can also be corroborated by other practitioners.

Do you believe in the Big Bang theory?

Actually, the explanation of the beginning of the universe given in the Vedic literature is not too dissimilar to that of modern science. But rather than a 'big bang', we have a 'big breath' as the universes (and there's more than one), looking like bubbles, each independent, come into being from a primordial 'steady-state' of non-material equilibrium. Eventually, after 311 trillion of our human years, the universes begin to drift back to the state in which they originated, each physical amalgamation separating into its constituent elements and each element being condensed into the next, more rarefied element until only the foundational pre-evolute or *pradhana* exists. Explained another way, the universes expand and drift away from the cosmic body of Vishnu who lies in a mystic slumber.

Do you believe in evolution?

We accept the phenomenon of evolution but do not believe that the mechanism offers either an explanation for the origin of species or the seemingly random nature of species development. Rather than reverse-extrapolating the principle of evolution to arrive at single-celled ancestors and their mathematically improbable destiny (as currently proposed), we accept the Vedic teaching of the origin of species. That is, the variety of living organisms show such a remarkable level of 'intelligent design' inherent in their information content and complexity, that to deny this element requires even more faith than religious belief itself. Evolution as a principle plays a large part in the general Vedic teaching of the beginnings of the universe, as it does when the progress of the soul through different species is examined.

But everyone seems to have a different idea of how to reach the spiritual bliss you're talking about; there are so many religions and they all say different things!

There are always two factors in a spiritual path: the exoteric and the esoteric. The exoteric means the external things, such as the language, the saint or prophet, the clothing, the particular writings of the tradition, the holy books and the detailed rules people follow. The internal, or esoteric, is the higher state of consciousness that is the aim of everything the followers do. If you analyse the highest aim of all religions, you'll find they all have much more in common than they have differences.

I don't know about that. It's a nice idea, but it seems like the arguments and fights between different religions these days are the cause of a lot of problems.

That's like saying your damp ceiling is the cause of a water leak. It's not. The damp ceiling is the symptom, not the cause. The real problem is a burst pipe in the attic. You have to go beyond the symptoms to find the cause. When a road breaks because of an earthquake, the cause is not the road itself, it's due to a release of pressure deep down in the Earth. The road just happens to be the fault line, the weakest dividing line between two places. The externals of ethnicity, tribe, language and religious identity are often the 'fault lines' along which communities split when there's a deeper disturbance.

So you don't agree that religious ideologies are the cause of many problems?

Non-religious ideologies are an even greater 'cause' of warfare and mass casualties. Of the 174 million deaths attributed to ideologies in the twentieth century, 92 million were due to non-religious ideas, such as communism and fascism. But I would like to reiterate—the problem is deeper than the surface.

If we knew the real problem, the world would be a more peaceful place. What's your idea?

The Bhagavad Gita says that there are three 'gates' leading to hellish consciousness from which hellish action flows—intense selfish desire, greed and anger. These three usually follow in a sequence. Rampant and uncontrolled desires to own, control and enjoy objects or people leads inevitably to greed for more of such things. When satisfaction proves unattainable, or when there are not enough resources for everyone's greed, there is frustration and subsequently anger. Once anger is in the system, it has to be discharged through thoughts, words or actions. Multiply that chain of events 1000 times and you'll have a world without peace.

But it seems that religions themselves are guilty of selfish desire, greed and anger!

Well, the humans who follow those religions—or who claim they follow them—are certainly guilty if they succumb to these three ancient enemies of peace. We have to know the signs of someone who is not overcome by these three. You don't have to be a great philosopher to understand it either. A person who is free from those will think, speak and act just the opposite. Instead of intense desire, there will be contentment with whatever he has, and instead of greed, he'll have a generous spirit to share what little he has with others. Instead of anger, there will be joy, and that, too, he'll share.

What's your definition of a 'tolerant religion'?

Academics who study religion divide all traditions in two—inclusive and exclusive. Because following a particular religion involves sticking to a body of ideas and practices, religious people adopt different stances to relate to others who do not follow the same ideas and practices.

So 'exclusive' is when a religious group considers that it has exclusive access to the truth, a revelation from God which is superior to others. It prefers to regard others as a challenge to their ideas, and practises and maintains a clear dividing line between themselves and others. The members might dress differently, minimize their social interactions and strive for 'purity' by separatism.

By contrast, the 'inclusive' religions regard God as one and His purpose as one, but His revelations as countless. They tend more to see the commonality between different religions, regarding the similarities between them as evidence of the singularity of God.

They do not feel threatened by the presence of others who do not share the same holy book, appearance or practices. As a result, they tend to be more tolerant of others.

Why are there so many religions if God is ultimately one?

The Bhagavad Gita explains that the path of yoga is the one true religion through which we can know and ultimately see God. But there are predominating forces of nature that cover the soul's vision of God. Sometimes, a cloud covers our eyes so that we can't see the sun. We say that the cloud has covered the sun, but it's our eyes that are the problem. We can see the hazy sunlight coming through the clouds, but not the sun directly.

In the same way, the soul is covered by the haze of layers of egotistic selfishness that prevent us from seeing God. This state then causes us to imagine a God according to our limited conception. We humans create many different religions due to our inability to see clearly. A multitude of spiritual teachers and leaders, saints, sages, and various 'sons' and 'prophets' of God come into the world. They appear at different places and times in history, and start teaching in the cultures that surround them. Then there are political intrigues as kings and rulers grasp religious messages to effect control of their citizens and change them in the process.

Hence, we end up with a wide variety of religions. Even the message of Jesus Christ—just one person—is now represented by no less than 47,000 different Christian sects. But remove many of the externals, and a great similarity of concept and purpose is revealed.

Do all paths lead to the same goal?

Imagine asking that question at a train station or an airport! They'd think you were slightly confused. But yes, in one sense, there is only one path—the path of God. Everyone is on that path, Lord Krishna says, and everyone has an equal chance to discover Him according to their level of surrender.

Yet, there are many ways that we can deviate from that one path and end up at different destinations. We can become sidetracked to the heavenly regions or we can descend to the hellish worlds. We can take birth again on this earth and suffer or enjoy the results of our deeds, or we can attain the 'white light' of the *Brahmajyoti* or merge into the cosmic ocean surrounding Vishnu if we choose to deny our individual existence. That's why it's important to have a guru, or spiritual teacher even if all paths lead to the same God.

7

Who Is Krishna?

Although the name 'Krishna' may sound familiar to many, it is unlikely that most have had the opportunity to truly comprehend the vastness that surrounds the term. Krishna is conceived by some as 'God' and by others as a mythological character from Eastern traditions. In ancient literature, Krishna's features affirm that Krishna is the original source of manifestations—both spirit and matter. Understanding why these wisdom books refer to Krishna not merely as 'God,' but as the 'Supreme Personality of Godhead', can change our outlook greatly. Specifically, one can gain invaluable insight into how the world functions, both outside of us and within.

Was Krishna human?

No. A human being is a spirit soul inside a material body. Krishna's body is spiritual, not material. Our body is made of material bones, muscles and blood, but the soul inside is spiritual. They are completely different—one is composed of matter and the other is spirit. Krishna's body is spirit all the way through. His body and soul are the same thing. Our bodies are born, last for 70–80 years and then disintegrate. That's because every material thing is a temporary combination of molecules and is in a state of perpetual flux. It comes into being in this specific formation, remains for some time and then disappears. Krishna's form always remains the same. It never becomes old and never changes. It is eternal. So Krishna is eternally in that form of Krishna, whether on the Earth 5000 years ago, today or 5000 years in the future. Those who think that He is like them don't understand Him, He says, because they imagine Him to be a mere human being with a body of flesh like theirs.

But Krishna has a human shape—doesn't that mean that someone has imagined Him?

It is the other way around. We have a 'Krishna shape'. Krishna isn't a creation of human beings who imagine a God shaped like them. Humans are a creation of a God shaped like Krishna. Imagining God to be like a human being is called anthropomorphism and understanding that we are shaped like God is called theomorphism—two very different ideas. Many people think that humans create God with their imagination, but it's the other way around—God creates us with His.

How do we really know what Krishna looks like?

So many people saw Krishna while He was on this planet for more than 100 years. There were millions of eyewitnesses. Images of Him were drawn and painted, and realistic sculptures were created. These were later installed in temples. Other than this, there was poetry written and detailed descriptions of the measurements of His divine form. These were then compiled—the measurements are still in use by members of the *shilpi* community, those who carve images from marble or mould them from bronze. But Krishna Himself has revealed His form and nature to sages and saints even before. How we now know is by studying all of the descriptions that appear in scriptures such as the Srimad Bhagavatam and Brahma Samhita. In the pages of those texts, there exist many detailed descriptions.

There are many different religions in the world. Why do you say they all worship Krishna?

Everyone who acknowledges the existence of God and worships Him actually worships Krishna, but some don't know Him by that name and form. When we say 'God', we mean the origin of creation, the all-pervading, supremely sentient, most powerful, beautiful, all-knowing and attractive person. By definition, there can only be one God because there can only be one origin of everything, one supreme source. Since everyone, by whatever name they call God, is indicating the same person, everyone worships Krishna in reality.

In the Bhagavad Gita, the Lord says that everyone is on the same path towards Him, but as they surrender to Him, He reveals Himself accordingly. Those who abandon all selfish interests are able to understand Krishna as He is.

But some religious people think of God as a mystery, or as a 'divine white light'. Are they wrong?

No, they are also right. If beauty, love, compassion, form and personality exist in this world, and if God is the origin of all of these, then surely, these attributes must be present within Him. The rays of the sun are made up of heat and light, and as such, the sun itself must possess heat and light. The closer you get towards the sun, the more heat and light you encounter. Therefore, the closer you move towards God, the more you experience the divine attributes. If one proposes that God is a mystery, it indicates that one doesn't know God, and if one sees God as a 'divine white light', it means that one has begun the journey towards Him. The divine white light is the preliminary stage of God-realization—the sunshine of the absolute Sun. As you progress towards Krishna, His personality is revealed.

Don't all religions take you to the same place?

Although everyone is on the same path, it may take many lifetimes for a person to become completely free from selfish desires. Along the way, one may attain the divine white light and spend thousands of years there before taking birth again. Or he may worship other powerful celestial beings—the demigods—and spend thousands of years with them before coming back down to this world. Taking birth into a rich family, one may become distracted by wealth and beauty. All of these obstacles delay a soul from finding its ultimate resting place.

If Krishna is a God of love, why does He send people to lower planets?

For the same reason that a government might send someone to prison—to safeguard the good people and reform the wayward. A prison is intended to be a place of change, where people can learn the error of their ways. The lower planets are also a place for learning lessons about our previous karmas. This situation is not permanent; it's a short chapter in the otherwise long book of life. Once the soul has been reformed in the lower planets, they return to the world to start again with a renewed perspective on life that is imprinted within the subconscious mind.

Why is Krishna blue?

Krishna has no cause. He is the cause of all causes. So there is no 'why' for anything that He is. Everything He is, and everything He does is perfect and complete. And if we adjust our perception to the reality of Krishna, we can directly become attracted to Him and rapidly make progress on our spiritual journey.

Why do some say that Krishna is immoral?

During His time on Earth, Krishna performed many compassionate deeds, such as protecting His devotees and subduing demons. But He also stole butter and the clothing of maidens while they were bathing, and danced with girls in the moonlight! But we would be wrong to conclude from this that Krishna is immoral or a hypocrite, asking us to follow rules that He doesn't follow.

The nature of the soul is infinitesimal and the nature of God is infinite. His position is eternal and unchanging, while our position keeps changing. We imagine ourselves to be God and, trapped inside temporary bodies, attempt to recreate the eternal enjoyment of God in a world whose very nature is changing. Krishna, or God, is the supreme enjoyer and we, the souls, are the enjoyed. Our attempts to change the parameters of this primeval relationship have been a failure. In order to regain our original position, we have to accommodate a new set of realities. God does not have to conform to the morality He requires of us, nor does He need to demonstrate it for our upliftment. Krishna is unchanging—we are the ones who are required to change.

Krishna asks everyone to bow down to Him—that doesn't seem to be humble.

It may seem as if Krishna is a supreme egotist, demanding our offerings, our meditation on Him and His name, and asking us to engage in conversations about Him or even to bow down to Him. We would not tolerate any human being making these demands of us. Rather, we would declare them to be a dictator. Why then should we accede to Krishna's requests? That would be a good question if Krishna was just another human being or a historical or imaginary figure. The truth is that He is none of these.

Krishna is, in fact, the only living entity qualified to ask us to do these things, and He asks not for Himself, but for us. Krishna doesn't need our bowing down, food, conversation or the recitation of His name.

Krishna only asks us to do anything at all because He is infinitely kind, and wants us to be completely free to be with Him and enjoy ourselves eternally. In order to qualify ourselves, we must train our self-centred consciousness to the level where we are conscious of God. And when we do that, we'll find that Krishna is not an egotist but our best friend.

I've heard we all have a specific relationship, or *rasa*, with Krishna. How can I know what rasa I have with Krishna?

Everything comes in its own time through the chanting of the Hare Krishna mantra:

Hare Krishna Hare Krishna
Krishna Krishna Hare Hare
Hare Rama Hare Rama
Rama Rama Hare Hare

Although the *mahamantra* is the mantra given to beginners on the path of bhakti, you should not think that it won't take you to the highest perfection. It is a mantra for the most spiritually advanced saints, which is why it is known as the 'great mantra'. In it, Krishna has invested all potencies. If you chant diligently, avoiding any offenses and bad habits, all possible results will come to you. At a certain point in your life, an intense pleasure will come as you chant. You won't even be able to imagine not chanting. After that, you will hear the sounds of the spiritual world. Then the features and activities of Krishna will become visible to you, along with your particular service, to one of His eternal devotees. In this way, your relationship with the Lord will be gradually revealed. There is no need for any additional training or mantras.

Why do you worship the guru like you worship God?

In many temples, you will also see a sacred statue, or *murti*, of the spiritual teacher or guru. Our founding spiritual teacher's full name is His Divine Grace Abhay Charanaravinda Bhaktivedanta Swami Prabhupada, or Srila Prabhupada for short. We do not worship him as God but as the servant of God. The pure devotee is dear to Krishna, having completely surrendered to Him, and through his blessings, we can come closer to Krishna as well. He is always with Krishna and serves Him eternally. Just as we might pray to Krishna, we also pray to the pure devotee of Krishna. Each morning, lamps, incense and flowers are also offered to him as part of a daily ceremony known as *guru puja*.

8

Gods and Demigods

One of the biggest mysteries to a spiritual seeker may be this: if God is just one, why are there many different religions and beliefs? Doesn't all this lead to mere confusion? And it gets even more complicated within the Vedic tradition itself, where one finds various 'Gods' and conflicts based on who's the greatest. If that isn't enough, there are even people who claim to be God. Actually, it's not at all complicated once we step back and take a bird's-eye view.

What is an incarnation?

The word *avatar* means 'one who descends', and refers to the forms that God takes when He enters this world to deliver the innocent and vanquish the evil. Although the English word 'incarnation' is used as a convenient translation, the Latin word actually means 'the spirit that comes into flesh'. This is not, however, how the Lord describes Himself. In the Bhagavad Gita, He says that He is never born and is not made of flesh and blood, and those who think Him to be just another human being are foolish. When Krishna comes to this world, He comes in His eternal form, in all His power, with the entire spiritual kingdom accompanying Him.

So, Krishna doesn't reincarnate?

No, it's just us that must be reincarnated! When we come into yet another womb of yet another mother, we are being reincarnated. We're being forced to take birth again and have no control over the matter. Due to our previous life's actions, we must enjoy and suffer once again. This is the real meaning of 'incarnation', or the 'spirit coming into the flesh'. Krishna does come into this world time after time. But in every case, He comes and goes as He pleases. He always remains in control of His destiny. Unlike us, He never becomes bewildered by the illusion of the world, even when He comes as a baby.

Who are the avatars of Vishnu?

There are as many avatars coming to this world as there are waves on a beach. There are lists of different incarnations of Vishnu, but the most common is a list of ten, which is as follows: Matsya (fish), Kurma (tortoise), Varaha (boar), Narsimha (half-man, half-lion), Vamana (dwarf), Parasurama (a warrior), Rama (a divine king), Balarama (Krishna's brother), Buddha (the enlightened one) and Kalki (the destroyer). Every avatar displays activities and speaks according to the specific needs of the circumstances of the world. In all forms, Lord Vishnu uplifts the *sadhus*, the people of good behaviour, while diminishing the power of the *duskritina*, those who are rebellious against God.

You say that Krishna is supreme, but surely Vishnu is supreme?

Vishnu and Krishna are the same reality in two forms. There is no competition between them. Only from our point of view do we consider it difficult to understand. Vishnu is God in the form of the creator and upholder of the universe, the indwelling witness and constant friend of the soul in the material world. Krishna is God who manifests His supremely attractive activities and beauty, and the One who invites all souls to come and join Him. These extra features constitute Krishna's superlative opulence, indicating His identity as the supreme, original personality of all Godhead. Just as an original candle flame can light many candles, Krishna is the original source of all incarnations. Overall, it could be said that Vishnu acts as 'God at work', and Krishna as 'God at home'.

Why do we need to worship Lord Chaitanya? Can I not just worship Krishna?

Chaitanya is none other than Krishna in the form of His own devotee. The Lord promises that He comes age after age to help establish dharma once again, and for the *Kali Yuga*, our present age, this is His form. So by worshipping Sri Chaitanya, you are directly worshipping Lord Krishna in a way that will attract even more blessings (since in the form of Chaitanya, Krishna is very kind to those who ask Him for help).

Why are there so many gods?

God is personal and the universe is personal. The gods—also known as devas, or demigods—are extremely powerful human beings with extraordinarily long lives, who are part of the universal administration. By themselves, they can award material benefits, but they can't give a soul freedom from samsara, or reincarnation. In fact, their many gifts to their worshippers only serve to prolong the souls' stay in the world. If we worship them at all, it is merely to acknowledge them as agents of the Supreme, Sri Krishna.

Who is Lord Jagannatha, the God with the big, round eyes?

That is also Krishna. There was once a king who was a great devotee, who asked a wood carver to fashion him statues of Krishna, Balarama and Their sister Subhadra as They appeared riding on chariots bound for a solar eclipse festival in Kurukshetra (the place where the Bhagavad Gita was spoken). The carver was interrupted and could not complete the forms, but the king worshipped Them anyway. They were painted black, white and yellow and stood some 8 feet high. A large temple was built for Them in Jagannatha Puri in eastern India. The three deities were placed on individual, brightly painted chariots, each with many wooden wheels. A large annual festival is held there now, where more than 2 million people come and pull the chariots through the streets. It is said that the large, unblinking eyes of Jagannatha are always open to give blessings to His devotees.

Why is God always born in India?

Although we might consider London or New York the most important places, it appears that God might have other ideas! The ancient scriptures talk of the

Himalayan mountains being the site of the beginnings of life on Earth, and the home of the greatest sages and yogis. India was certainly civilized at a time when human society was only sparsely distributed elsewhere. God can appear anywhere He likes, naturally, and He has certainly sent His sons and saints to other places on the planet. But due to the many appearances of Krishna in the land now known as India, there exist hundreds of places of pilgrimage where beautiful temples are visited and saintly devotees gather. We can all take advantage of this by going on pilgrimage, or *yatra*, at least once in our lifetime.

9

Holy Books and Hinduism

A lot of religions, including the Vedic tradition, seem to rely on information based on ancient books that were written many thousands of years ago. One may question the value of relying on sources whose authenticity we cannot even trace when it comes to tangible historical evidence. As it happens, many important books in different traditions have been interpolated. Couldn't that be the case with the Vedic books too? Even if it were all true and faultless, why do so many books exist, and how do they fare in terms of authenticity on a spiritual level? Written for different audiences to help them relate to the spiritual contexts effectively, different books provide us with interesting insights into our relationship with the divine.

What are the Puranas?

Purana means 'ancient history' and refers to the scriptures that give accounts of the beginnings of the universe, the origins of the gods, the dynasties of great kings and saints, and the many avatars of Vishnu and His wonderful deeds. There are eighteen major Puranas, the chief of which is the Bhagavata Purana, otherwise known as the Srimad Bhagavatam.

What about the Mahabharata and the Ramayana—are they also part of the Vedas?

These are known as *itihasa*, or history, but they are constructed in a slightly different way. The Ramayana is an extended account of the avatar of Lord Rama. It was compiled by the great sage Valmiki in 24,000 verses and is known as the first poem. Rama is known as *Maryada purushottama*. The word *maryada* means a demarcation line between two areas, like the one Lord Rama carefully marked to differentiate between good and bad actions, leaving a great legacy of life guidance for generations to come.

The Mahabharata is a history of the major events surrounding two great dynasties. At its heart is the battle of Kurukshetra with the dialogue between Krishna and Arjuna forming the philosophical centrepiece, spoken just before the great battle. The Mahabharata has 1 lakh verses and was compiled by the greatest of all sages, Srila Vyasa Deva. These two works are filled with Vedic wisdom. Together with the Puranas, they are therefore considered to be *Panchama Veda*, or the 'Fifth Veda'.

I have heard there are two holy books, Shruti and Smriti—why are there two?

These are not two holy books, but one body of scripture from two sources. *Shruti* means 'that which is heard', and refers to the knowledge that was heard from God Himself in the beginning of creation. The Lord also revealed the original Veda to great gods and yogis. Sometime later in the creation, the Lord spoke again. His teachings and glorious actions were remembered by the greatest saints, who put the accounts of His deeds into their own words. This body of work is known as *Smriti*, meaning 'that which is remembered'. Both types of texts are considered equally sacred and are not in competition with each other

Do people on the path of Bhakti study any other books?

Well, in addition to the two main texts of Bhagavad Gita and Srimad Bhagavatam, we also study the teachings of Krishna's incarnation of Chaitanya Mahaprabhu. Krishna came in the mood and form of His own devotee to teach the essence of religion 500 years ago, and had thousands of followers all over India. Some of those followers lived in Vrindavan, Krishna's original home. The most famous were a group of six perfected devotees known as the Goswamis. Now, we study Chaitanya Mahaprabhu's teachings and life, and the six Goswami's philosophical writings. Rupa Goswami wrote the *Bhakti-Rasamrita-Sindhu*, now translated into English as *The Nectar of Devotion*. Later on, a follower of the six Goswamis, named Krishnadas, wrote a detailed biography of Chaitanya Mahaprabhu. He named it *Chaitanya Charitamrta* and we also study this regularly.

What are the other schools of philosophy in India?

There are so many that it would take years to describe them all! The schools of philosophy are like the many branches of a tree. Although the branches may be many, spreading in different directions, they all receive nourishment from the same trunk and roots. Lord Krishna spoke to such great devotees as Brahma, Shiva, Narada Muni, Sri Lakshmi and so on, and then those teachings were passed down through a chain of teachers and students.

Over time, slight differences of emphasis arose in the teachings and different schools of philosophy developed. But each group can trace their origins to the Vedas. In some cases, one or two schools have rejected the Vedas as their scriptural authority, preferring the mystical teaching of their particular saint. Both Jainism and Buddhism, also originating in India, are in this category.

It seems very complex—how do we reconcile the different schools of philosophy?

The questions you have to ask any school of philosophy are these: What is your ultimate goal? How will you get there? Who is the founder of your school of thought? The answers to these questions will help you understand the authenticity and spiritual authority of the community. There are three ultimate goals proposed by any of the schools—the extinction of the self, the merging of the self and the eternal devotion of the self. Or to put it simply: 0-1-2. Thus, all the schools of philosophy in India can be explained as the school of zero, the school of oneness and the school of the eternal relationship. The other details will be of philosophical emphasis, technique, original teacher and culture.

So you read the Vedas and worship Krishna—it sounds like you are Hindus?

The actual word 'Hindu' doesn't appear anywhere in the original scriptures of India. Nowhere in the Vedas or Bhagavad Gita does it mention 'Hinduism'. The word seems to have been given by Persians and Greeks who came into what is now India and encountered people living by the Indus River. The British then came and added the '-ism' to the word 'Hindu'. But now the term has stuck.

You don't like the word 'Hindu?'

We prefer the term 'Sanatana Dharma' because it more accurately describes the eternal path spoken of in the scriptures. Hinduism is a broad term, one that means so many different things to different people. Historically speaking, from the time it was first used, it was a word that indicated those who had not submitted to Islam. Since clarity of terminology makes things more understandable for everyone and understanding anything is so important in the world today, we prefer Sanatana Dharma.

Is there a 'Hindu trinity'?

The expression 'Hindu trinity' originally came from Christian missionaries in India. The Christian trinity of 'father, son and holy spirit' is a theological concept indicating the One God who appears in three aspects. Looking for similarities in the concepts of the Hindus, the Christians looked at Brahma, Vishnu and Shiva, and called them a trinity accordingly. They got it wrong. In reality, there is one Supreme God, Vishnu, and two demigods of differing powers, Brahma and Shiva. They are both generated from Vishnu and gain their powers from Him. However, these three do share the three aspects of universal creation, maintenance and destruction.

In chronological sequence, Vishnu creates Brahma, and then Brahma generates Shiva. In the cosmic order, Brahma creates the universe, Vishnu as the all-pervading soul of the universe maintains it and, when the time is right, Shiva destroys it. For these functions, and these functions only, they are known as the three *guna-avatars*, or incarnations of the qualitative modes of nature—passion (*rajas*), goodness (*sattva*) and ignorance (*tamas*). But the term 'trinity' tends to suggest that they are merely three aspects of one impersonal Supreme, which is a common misconception.

What is meant by the word *moksha*?

The word 'moksha' means release, liberation and complete freedom from all suffering. For the soul to be trapped in the never-ending chain of death followed by rebirth, followed again by death, is the worst form of suffering. Moksha means that the soul breaks free from this cycle. One form of moksha is to enter into the Brahma-jyoti, the 'white light' and the great spiritual energy that permeates everything. Unfortunately, this is also temporary, even though the freedom enjoyed by the soul lasts for many thousands of years. Ultimate moksha means to enter into the realm of Vaikuntha. There, having awakened our eternal relationship with the Supreme, we can reside forever.

If the entire world was influenced by Vedic culture in ancient times, why did it disappear?

The Vedic culture was based on the knowledge of the Vedas. Modern research suggests that it was known from the present-day Mediterranean and Middle East through the Himalayan cultures and India to Burma, Thailand, Cambodia and Singapore. Architectural and linguistic evidence of the worship of Vishnu has been found in Russia and China. As time went by, different kings and rulers took aspects of the Vedic culture and applied it to their citizens, in their own climatic and political circumstances. In different parts of the world, we can see how the Vedic language has lingered, often disguised by thousands of years of history. For instance, the word *veda* meaning 'to know' gives us the word *vidya* or knowledge, which then becomes *videre* in Latin, meaning 'to know', and *video*, meaning 'I see'. There's a similar relationship with the Sanskrit word for God: *deva*. From this came the Latin *deo*, the Old French *dieu* and even the Welsh *duw*—all words meaning the supreme person. The ancient practice of fire ceremonies described in the Vedas may also have entered our language. The Sanskrit for fire is *Agni*, from which comes the Latin *igneo*, giving us the English word *ignite*. The name for gods are similarly related, the Sanskrit *dyu pita* or 'father of the gods' became the Latin Jupiter, the father of the gods.

How did so many religions come about?

According to the Vedas, religion is composed of *yagya*, or the sacrifice of materially enjoyable things for a higher purpose. *Dana* refers to giving to others in charity, while *tapa* or penance is the act of taking on voluntary restriction or personal disciplines so that the soul can break free from the mind's urges and the demands of the senses. All religions contain these elements, although the founder of the religious tradition may have expressed it in different ways, to different degrees, and according to the time, place and circumstances of the people. If we examine the numerous religions of the world, we find that they all originated at a historical time when they were needed by the people of a particular region. Although the external elements may differ, such as clothing, language and leadership, the essential messages are very similar.

Do I need to be a philosopher to join Hare Krishna?

You don't need any qualifications apart from your enthusiasm. But philosophy will help you to clarify your thoughts, see what's logical and sensible, and give you the intellectual conviction to sustain your faith. As soon as you've become convinced, philosophy has done its initial job. Along the way, though, it is essential to learn the details of Krishna and how your relationship with Him can be cultivated. This isn't philosophy as such, but theology, the study of God. This type of knowledge will keep you sharp and prevent your faith from fading.

Does it bother you that you won't have enough life to learn all the scriptures?

There are as many scriptures as there are grains of sand on a beach. You would need many lifetimes to learn everything. But the essence of everything is contained in just one book, the Bhagavad Gita. In this one conversation of 700 beautiful verses, the Lord teaches the conclusion of the four Vedas, the essence of the Upanishads and the final word of the Puranas.

Why does it say 'As It Is' on Srila Prabhupada's translation of the Bhagavad Gita?

There are many translations of Bhagavad Gita, including hundreds in English. Very few of them provide the deeper meanings of the message of Krishna, which include directions on transcendental devotional service, culminating in the Lord's final instructions to—'Always think of Me and become My devotee. Worship Me and offer your homage unto Me. Thus you will come to Me without fail. Abandon all varieties of religion and just surrender unto Me. I shall deliver you from all sinful reactions. Do not fear.' In addition, Srila Prabhupada's commentaries to each verse are based on the authoritative words of generations of great teachers before him. This makes the 'As It Is' version complete and one of the bestselling Gitas in the world today.

But how can one be sure it's the correct understanding?

They say that the proof of the pudding is in the eating, so the fact that people have become devotees in so many lands is proof that they have understood Krishna correctly. Aside from this, the *Bhagavad Gita As It Is* contains the full Devanagari Sanskrit script (the original language of the Gita), the word meanings, detailed translations and full commentary. It is, by far, the most thorough and detailed version of the Gita available. Besides this, the teachings of the Bhagavad Gita have been passed down through the centuries from guru to disciple, so that the message has been preserved intact.

The line of gurus given in the front pages of *Bhagavad Gita As It Is*—is it complete?

There are some historical gaps between several of the gurus. It sometimes happens in history that the sublime teachings of bhakti become lost. Even Lord Krishna says that He has to come to this world from time to time in order to restore dharma. So the line of gurus or teachers that represent Him occasionally becomes fractured for one reason or another. But just as a river may sometimes go underground only to rise again miles away, the pure stream of knowledge occasionally disappears only to rise again some years later.

But haven't the teachings been gradually changed due to so many gurus in the chain?

Luckily, there are many ways in which teachings can be preserved. Because the Vedic teachings are based upon an oral tradition, there were extensive methods of correcting pronunciation and keeping the sounds of the mantras accurate. Later, Srila Vyasa Deva saw that people's memories in the future would grow weak, so he compiled everything and wrote it down.

Where is the original Bhagavad Gita—the manuscript?

The oldest Bhagavad Gita is in the Wellcome Trust Museum in London. It is dated 1488, which is not very old in Indian terms. We don't know if there is an original manuscript anywhere since they were written on leaves.

It is also sad to report that in India, many old manuscripts were destroyed by invading armies and many more were thrown away simply because they were old! Now, many Bhagavad Gitas have been inscribed on copper, buried in time capsules or sealed in bombproof mountain caves. We are taking no chances for the next generations!

Aren't the stories in the scriptures just helpful myths?

It's interesting how we regard events we believe to be true as 'history' and those we can't comprehend as 'mythology'. The two terms have more to say about our level of acceptance than the veracity of the incidents. There are many phenomena we have not personally witnessed, even in this world, and our experience of reality is therefore highly circumscribed.

Infrared and ultraviolet lights are beyond our perception, making anything that emits them outside our spectrum of visible phenomena. Our eyes cannot even perceive the things that lesser creatures like insects can see. How then do we propose to claim to know what is real and what is myth?

While people can, and do, create stories about men and women with superpowers, we should be careful of what we deny. The reality of the universe may be more wonderful than we can presently conceive.

Scripture employs much metaphorical and poetic speech in order to illustrate philosophical points. But there is a distinction between these and accounts of historical events, which may be beyond our conception. We have to know which is metaphor and which is history, and the difference between them is usually explained in the text itself.

10

Active Spirituality

Some of the most challenging questions spiritual practitioners face are those dealing with the application of scriptural knowledge in everyday life. Although the spiritual aphorisms contained within the books may hold great value, it is the implementation of these that actually qualifies the understanding behind it. Some aspects may even sound counter-intuitive to everyday moral concerns. Yet, when we study them deeper and practice them with sincerity, we realise that the theory and practice only complement and support one another.

What are the main things that I need to do to be spiritual?

There are thousands of things you could do to lead a more spiritual life. But if you want practical suggestions of the best things that will give you results quickly, then just remember these letters: **A B C D E F G.**

A is for Association. Whatever you keep company with—the food, music, books, movies, television, websites and newspapers you consume, your phone conversations, your work colleagues—are what you associate with. By choosing carefully, you can create a favourable environment for your mind and a great foundation for spiritual life. Be with positive people who lift you up and give you positive, life-affirming thoughts. Avoid those who don't.

B is for Books. Whatever you read becomes a voice in your head, and will affect how you see the world and make choices of direction. Books like the Gita and Bhagavatam are full of powerful spiritual messages that will help you see the world around you from the soul's point of view.

C is for Chanting. Although we all have to work late nights these days, it's worth getting to bed earlier, waking up slightly earlier and getting in some morning mantra meditation before breakfast. Chanting of the maha mantra is the greatest way to experience a quite remarkable transformation of consciousness. Do it regularly and you'll never look back.

D is for Diet. The path of Bhakti yoga begins with the tongue, with chanting and sacred food. If you avoid three types of food, you'll feel better, create no karma and become connected with Krishna:

(a) Foods that are the product of violence, such as red meat, poultry, fish, lobster, crab and shellfish.
(b) Foods that are considered impure, such as eggs (whether fertilized or not), and some fungi.
(c) Foods that agitate the mind, such as onions, garlic, alcohol, chilli and foods with high sugar.

E is for Enthusiasm. You'll do well on the spiritual path if, once you've decided it's for you, you throw yourself into it with all your enthusiasm and without reservation. Don't wobble or waver in your spiritual life—be determined and enthusiastic.

F is for Friends. We all have an intimate circle of friends. They're the ones who support you through hard times, visit you in the hospital and care about what you're into. For rapid spiritual growth, we'd recommend having at least two spiritual friends in this inner circle, or more if you can. Why? Because we tend to listen to our close friends, and if they are also practising Bhakti yoga, it's a powerful friendship to have.

G is for Group. You can join a group for any interest under the sun. Weekly or monthly group meeting helps to keep your interest alive. There's probably a Bhakti yoga group very near you. You'll learn more, have fun and find inspiration. You'll be taking part in kirtan, talks and discussions, and if there's a free meal at the end of it, that's another problem solved.

Why do you put such an emphasis on chanting?

The main practice in awakening our spiritual nature is the turning around of our consciousness from self-centred to God-centred. It involves offering our words, wealth, time and intelligence to God. Some of this is done as part of daily life while some is done in powerful ritualized practices.

Vedic cosmology describes four great epochs of time, rotating one after the other in an endless cycle spanning millions of years. In each of these cosmic seasons, known as *yugas*, one distinct yogic practice enables rapid spiritual progress. In the first epoch, known as the Satya age, the best form of yoga is meditation on Vishnu in the heart; in Treta, it is fire sacrifices; in Dwapara, opulent temple ceremonies; and in Kali Yuga, the present age, the prescribed method is the congregational singing of the names of Hari (Vishnu).

Indeed, the Brihan-Naradiya Purana says, '*Harer-namaiva kevalam* [the chanting of the holy name of Hari (Krishna) is the only way]'. When Sri Chaitanya appeared in India, He promoted the chanting of the names of Krishna as both a personal practice, and a collective, congregational and musical practice. The result of His teachings and of those who followed Him is the modern-day Hare Krishna movement.

Why do you worship idols?

The 'idols', as you call them, are the essential point of focus within a temple. Although the Abrahamic faiths proscribe the worship of 'graven images' and subject anyone who does so to punishment, it is important to understand the reasoning behind this form of worship. Firstly, it should be noted that imaginary images are forbidden in the Vedic tradition. No good can come from worshipping an imaginary God. An artist cannot simply create an image and ask everyone to bow down to it. The devotees of Krishna are in complete agreement with Judaism, Christianity and Islam on this point.

But God, since He is the origin of all forms, does have an actual form, and this revealed form can be worshipped. The rule is that the form of the temple must be made according to descriptions given in sacred scriptures. The form of God, when fashioned in a material element such as wood, stone or metal, and according to the sacred texts, is then installed with authorized rituals and mantras. God can turn spirit into matter and matter into spirit, so His consecrated statue should never be mistakenly identified as being made of matter. The sacred image is one way that the invisible and untouchable God makes Himself available to the senses of the devotee. Instead of the English word 'idol', we can instead use the correct terms of *archa-murti* or 'worshippable form'.

If you are spiritual, why do you use technology?

We would much prefer that the messages of Krishna were already heard, understood and honoured all over the world. Our motto is 'simple living, high thinking,' and we much prefer sustainable, natural devices to technological ones. But since we would like the entire world to learn about the teachings of Krishna, we are taking the opportunity to use any invention to disseminate the information. Devotees of Krishna thus run radio stations, both analogue and digital, television studios and naturally produce millions of books—both in print and electronic formats. At the same time, we also create sustainable communities where members can live off the land, and horses and oxen provide transport.

Why do you spend so much money on temples? Why not use it to help others?

Temples and the worship that goes on inside them have a powerful and positively uplifting effect on people. For this reason, in any major European city, you'll find that the cathedral or church is right in the middle of the population. From the religious centre came education, medical care, hospice facilities, food distribution and help for the poor, morality, arts and culture (music, writing, architecture), and many other aspects of progressive society. In India, it was the same; the temples performed unlimited amounts of social service.

I always thought that meditation was done silently, with closed eyes. Is that so?

The most ancient forms of authentic meditation have always involved the recitation of sound formulas, or mantras, which may be spoken out loud, murmured, or heard within the mind with no sound at all. The meditation known as *japa*—the repetition of the Hare Krishna mantra—is actually far more absorbing than silent meditation. Proof of this is that a regular chanter can meditate for two hours at a time. Silent meditation simply means that an observer cannot hear a sound, but the meditator can. After the advent of Buddhism in India, other forms of meditation developed, which later spread to Tibet, China and Japan. Many of them also involve focusing the mind on sound. It is difficult—almost impossible—to focus on nothing.

Why is a mantra more purifying than any other sound?

A mantra is a spiritual sound vibration. Its origins are not in the world of matter. All mantras come from God and have been passed down by a chain of *rishis* (seers) and gurus (teachers). Although when listening to a mantra, we only hear syllables made by the tongue and vibrated as sound waves, it would be incorrect to think that the syllables themselves are the sum total of the mantra. The sounds are invested with potency beyond our imagination. Their true power becomes evident upon chanting with attention.

Do I have to give away all my money to be a devotee?

The Isha Upanishad says that everything is controlled and owned by the Lord, but that we can use what we have been allotted as per our quota. If we remember those facts and work in that consciousness, we may live happily for 100 years. So we have a right to transform our God-given talents into hard work and success, but the fruits of the work belong to God. We are allowed to use them, as long as we are mindful of His ownership.

Wealth and poverty are therefore neutral—you are not closer to God by being poor or further away from Him by being rich. You are closer to Him by using whatever you have in His service. You can give your money to a good cause, particularly a saintly person or a temple, or you can do God's work in the world and become a saintly person yourself!

Why are there 108 beads on a set of the Hare Krishna meditation beads, the *japa-mala*?

There are so many occurrences of the number 108 in ancient civilization that it is difficult to know where to begin. In mathematics, 108 is considered an 'abundant' number* and one with which a small computation produces the golden ratio.† In ancient mathematics, it was considered an auspicious number. In modern astronomy, the ratio of the diameters of the sun, moon and earth are all calculated to be an average of 108. There are 108 pressure points in the body according to the Indian martial art *Marma Adi*. There are said to be 108 Upanishads. And of course, it is said that Lord Krishna had 16,108 queens. The number 108

* First described in 100 AD in *Introductio Mathematica* compiled by Nichomachus, an abundant number is a positive integer for which the sum of its proper divisors. is greater than the number.

† Golden ratio, or the divine proportion, is a ratio between two numbers that equals approximately 1.618. Also known as the Fibonacci sequence, this ratio appears throughout nature and is employed in architecture, sculpture and paintings.

also adds up to nine in numerology, the number of the guru principle.

There are 108 holy places in Vaishnavism and of course, 108 beads on a set of japa-mala.

11

Food and Diet

It is said that what we eat affects not just how we look but also how we think. What you eat becomes you—since food is what we're made of, at least on the bodily level. Therefore, it makes sense to be sensible about our dietary intake. Some people argue, however, for the consumption of designated levels of alcohol and meat, in order to maintain the body's needs for a balanced diet and the mind's needs for sanity. However, the Vedic tradition looks at the physical, mental and spiritual needs of everyone, and explains why certain things are not just unnecessary, but also counterproductive for our well-being. To summarize, consumption of healthy, meat-free and intoxicant-free foods helps us become nourished.

Why are devotees vegetarian?

There are so many reasons! Where should we begin? Firstly, we practise *ahimsa* or non-violence, so we don't kill animals for food or pay others to do it for us—be it butchers or fast-food chains. Eating meat is both cruel and unnecessary. There is no good reason to eat animals for food; there are so many other sources of protein and minerals. Good old-fashioned rice and dal, for instance, when mixed, can provide all the essential amino acids that boost protein in your body. The meat industry, which is responsible for the wastage of precious land, water and transport fuel, is also the highest producer of greenhouse gases. We can all do without this. The main reason for devotees being vegetarian is that we only eat food that has been offered first to Krishna—*prasadam*—and Krishna does not want to eat dead animals.

You're still killing plants when you're vegetarian, aren't you?

Yes, killing is required with vegetables but not with fruits. Since life is sustained by life, and we must continue to live, we must take life from something. But in doing so, we must choose foods that involve the least amount of pain possible. Plants are much less sentient than an animal with a spinal cord. In addition, plants can be offered to Krishna.

Why do you not eat eggs?

Eggs are a product of the menstrual cycle of the chicken. Whether fertilized or unfertilized, we do not eat them because they are not considered clean.

What's so bad about onions and garlic?

Although tasty for some tongues, these two vegetables contain oils that are not conducive to maintaining a fixed level of meditation. They make the mind wander, even when you are trying to fix it at one point. Consequently, anyone whose job role requires a good level of concentration would do well to avoid them.

What's wrong with mushrooms?

If you pick them yourself, and you make sure you're picking the non-poisonous variety, there is no harm. But, fungi are also considered to be in the food group that tends to cloud the mind and reduce the capability of clear thought.

And what about alcohol—not even at weddings or celebrations?

There was a time when no one at a Vedic wedding ceremony would even have dreamed of drinking alcohol. It wasn't considered necessary to have a good time. Now all types of alcohol are widely available and served at functions, and being a non-drinker is considered something unusual. Just in one generation! Alcohol is always bad news and regularly wrecks families, destroys livers and causes addictive behaviour, resulting in loss of promotions and a successful career. Just make a promise to your children to avoid it and see what a difference it makes.

Someone told me devotees don't drink tea and coffee. Is that true?

That someone was correct! Although they are only mild intoxicants, they are unhelpful to the system, overstimulate the brain and produce an acidic after-effect, which is the foundation of disease. Their over-cultivation in some countries destroys the fine balance of agriculture, leading to food deprivation.

Please don't tell me that I can't even eat chillies!

All right, I won't. But I will tell you that over-consumption of chillies inflames the stomach and the blood circulation and leads to inattention. It enhances the *raja-guna*—the passions—making you irritable and anxious at work and with your family. But I didn't say you couldn't eat them.

Why do you drink cow's milk if you don't eat beef?

Milk can give us all the ingredients of meat without ever having to harm the cow. We believe in a mutually helpful relationship between humans and cows. The bulls plough the fields and provide transport, and the cows provide milk, which can be made into yoghurt, butter and ghee. In return, humans can protect cows as they would their other pets. Milk is a wonder food with several health-giving properties.

But most cows are factory-farmed and their calves are killed. Why do you use commercial dairy milk if it's the product of such cruelty?

You are right about factory farming and milk bought from the supermarket. Our response has been to create our own farms where our cows can live out their lives without any cruelty. Such milk is *ahimsa*, or non-violent. Of course, this way of caring for cows cannot be undertaken by everyone, but we would like to see it more widespread. We do produce some ahimsa milk for sale, but not enough that everyone can choose to have it. So some of our members have decided to avoid commercial milk altogether; others offer milk to Krishna in the understanding that both the giver and receiver of the milk will be purified by this devotional offering.

What's your message to the world?

For us, human life is all about gradually waking up to our spiritual nature and working towards spiritual freedom. Everything else should serve that end. When spiritual needs are given priority, everything else can be achieved—peace, food, water, prosperity, education. We can all help each other by working on our compassion and respect for others. To do that, we need to understand that happiness can't be gained from an incessant march towards greater levels of materialism. Without that basic understanding, we'll compete with others for limited resources, over-indulge at the expense of other communities and eventually fight with them.

To overcome this tendency takes *yagya*—the spirit of sacrifice. Our message is that much of this can be accomplished if we join together in kirtan, the joyful singing of mantras. We humbly ask everyone: 'Please chant Hare Krishna and be happy'. So self-realization, spiritual freedom, compassion, respect, personal restraint, sacrifice and singing together are a few values we believe in—that is our message to the world.

What would you change if you could?

One of our principles is 'simple living, high thinking'. It's based on the idea that when you simplify your basic needs, you'll find the time for more important activities. There is much about modern life that is unnecessarily complex. Finding somewhere to live has been made needlessly hard with planning and building restrictions and the housing market, for example.

Working at what you love is becoming difficult, and education often means training for a career that may not exist in a few years. Even eating has now been made dependent on factories and vast transportation networks. We believe that we've gone quite far enough with social complexity. The petrol-driven, industrialized society is now dangerously short-term.

There are many practical and spiritual benefits if we can simplify our approach to basic essentials. Food can be grown locally and transported at a minimal distance only. Smaller towns and villages can become the norm, and the growth of overcrowded, polluted cities can be reduced. Our animal-based diet and level of consumption are cruel and unsustainable, and a plant-based diet is much healthier.

We can keep food real, and do away with all the unnatural flavourings and additives as well as the fats and sugars that make us all unhealthy. A shift from sedentary, machine-based occupations to ones where we use our innate propensities and skills would keep us all happily engaged and rewarded.

12

Appearance and Lifestyle

People often question whether one needs to change one's appearance in order to develop a deeper relationship with the divine. Although one's spiritual connection with the divine may not depend upon adopting a particular attire, it definitely helps one feel part of the community of practitioners that may impact one's spiritual practice. Being part of a community is essential for spiritual progress because we can learn, practise and grow, based on where we're situated in society. Vedic tradition has many different attires to facilitate one's spiritual experience, and just understanding this can give us insights into the depth of devotional practice contained within. Philosophy and thinking are necessary. Now let's talk a bit about some practicalities. On a day-to-day basis, what will help me in my practice of spiritual life? How much can I realistically do at home? Are there different times of day for spiritual practice? What about sleeping—I heard you all get up really early. Why is that?

What do male devotees wear?

Some male devotees wear the traditional robe, known as a dhoti. It's one piece of cloth, five metres long, cotton or silk, sometimes jute, and can be folded in different ways. It's worn for simplicity—both in the production of the garment and the wearing of it. It's warmer than it looks, and comfortable too. It's worn with a kurta, and there's a matching shawl known as a *chaddar*. A thicker shawl made of wool is often worn on cooler days.

Should I wear a dhoti when I visit the temple?

You can wear whatever is clean and smart and comfortable, but if you'd like to wear a dhoti, why not? You could try wearing one on special occasions and might even like it. In southern India, it's very common to see men wearing them, in the north less so. But now they are worn all over the world.

What is the meaning behind the haircut the men have?

The lock of hair is known as the *sikha*. This translates as 'summit' or sometimes 'flag'—like the top of a temple dome with the flag flying. Shaving the head is said to reduce vanity, and the sikha reminds the wearer that his own body is itself a type of temple. The monks and some of our other members like to wear their hair like that. The sikha is a requirement for conducting all types of sacred rituals.

Why do you have that mark on your forehead?

The mark is known as tilak or *pundra*, and it's made of a kind of yellow clay known as *gopi-chandan*. The twin lines on the forehead are said to depict the outline of Krishna's foot and the mark on the nose represents a leaf of the sacred tulasi tree. In India, there are many different varieties of pundra, each revealing the religious community of the wearer. Tilak markings are another way the devotee is reminded that the body belongs to Krishna.

What do women wear?

Many women like to wear traditional saris. The main point is to dress in what you feel is appropriate for a sacred space.

Some people wear orange. What does that mean?

Those are the monks. After a period of preparation, some men, usually younger, opt to live a simple life of discipline, including celibacy. They practise their spiritual life as a religious community and can often be seen working hard around the temple, performing worship on the main altar or teaching classes.

Can they get married?

Yes, this form of celibate life comes with the option of getting married if that becomes more suitable. In that case, the devotee goes from the life of the *brahmachari*, or monk, to the married life of the *grihasta*.

I have seen a monk carrying an orange stick—what is that?

That stick is actually a bundle of three bamboo sticks tied together and then wrapped in saffron-coloured cloth. It is carried by a special type of monk known as a *sannyasi*—one who has opted for lifetime celibacy and an itinerant lifestyle, travelling to many places to give the teachings to others. The three sticks indicate that he has formally dedicated his actions, thoughts and words to Krishna.

Why do women have to cover their hair?

They are not obliged to, but it is customary in many traditional cultures for women to cover their most attractive features when in the presence of monks. Some women tie back their hair, and others choose to cover it with the end of their sari or a scarf. It is not a rule, however, merely an optional and additional observance.

You said that orange means a monk; what does white mean?

White is simply the colour of bleached cotton. It has no other significance. Many married men wear white, but they are not restricted from wearing any other colour they choose. Single men who are new students in the community may also wear white or yellow.

Who can give classes or lead the singing in the temple?

Anyone who is a committed follower can lead the singing, and anyone who is sufficiently knowledgeable, and who has adequately prepared, may be invited to deliver a class on the Bhagavad Gita in the evening. Giving the morning class is a service reserved principally for the senior members.

I hear devotees talking about the 'modes of nature'. What are they?

The word 'mode' is an English rendition of the Sanskrit word *guna*, meaning 'rope'. According to Vedic metaphysics, matter or *prakriti* is constantly in a state of flux, with the elements combining and disintegrating through time and space. The primordial constituents of matter are three qualities known as sattva, rajas and tamas. Rajas, or passion, pushes matter into fresh combinations; sattva, or goodness, holds matter in a steady state; and tamas, ignorance or darkness, slows down combinations and disintegrates. Correspondingly, these three influence the ego of an individual, which affects the equilibrium, pushing the mind and senses toward clarity, inspiration, creativity and harmony (sattva); agitation, desire, restlessness and worry (rajas); or inertia, doubt, boredom and fear (tamas). All contact between the senses and their objects is also constituted of mixtures of these three modalities.

How can we know what modes will influence us and when?

The three modes of nature are as regular as clockwork—literally. In fact, the cycle of the three modes is what makes up each day. Twenty-four hours contain three periods of eight hours each. Within each period of eight hours, the respective mode grows in intensity reaching a high point and then fading as the next mode begins to predominate. The influence of the mode of goodness grows in intensity from midnight, peaks at 4 a.m. and then diminishes to 8 a.m. when passion takes over, growing in dominance until its midpoint around midday.

It can be noted that tendencies toward creativity and energy expenditure take place at certain times, as does relaxation and sleep, or nighttime enjoyment and indolence. Those who wish to take advantage of the best possible time for spiritual activity can rise at 4 a.m. to make the most of the 'golden period' for meditation (known as the *brahmamuhurtha*), which lasts for forty-eight minutes and begins ninety-six minutes before the astronomical sunrise.

Why is it necessary to have a cold shower?

First of all, having a quick shower first thing in the morning, or as the devotees say, 'taking a bath', is an essential ingredient of the Bhakti yoga lifestyle. After sleeping for eight hours or so, washing off the toxins of the night helps you to collect your thoughts and get ready for meditation. A cold splash after your warm shower will not only close your pores (good for health) and completely wake you up but also allow you to stay awake through your all-important meditation hour.

What else do the devotees do in the morning?

A quite common preparation for the day is using the *thuli*, less attractively known as the 'tongue-cleaner'. It's a one-centimetre wide, U-shaped band of steel which is drawn down over the extended tongue, cleaning it of the night's toxins. Devotees also like to drink warm water in the morning, often with added lemon juice. This helps with hydration and 'keeping things like clockwork'. You might find other devotees practising a few minutes of yoga *asanas*[*] in the morning, in addition to all their regular chanting and reading, of course. Some breathing exercises or *pranayama* are always helpful to focus the mind before chanting, removing any memories of dreams the night before.

Things devotees don't do in the early morning include checking their phones, listening to the radio or reading the newspaper. From the time they wake up (usually to the sound of an alarm clock or digital equivalent) right up until breakfast, devotees are engaged in devotion. They know that this is the most important part of the day, the part that prepares them for everything else the day will bring.

The devotee's 'morning programme' might run from before 4 a.m. until 8.30 a.m. Those who commute to work or get children ready for school would have to adjust their schedule accordingly, but the same level of focus and commitment to setting aside sacred time is required of all serious practitioners.

* A series of sitting postures to aid the flow of 'subtle airs' or *prana* within the body, thereby supporting meditation practice.

13

Vedic Perspectives

Religion seems to be responsible for a tremendous amount of violence in the world. Could Krishna's consciousness ever be violent? Isn't it better just to help people than to spread yet another religion? Why do many religions look down on women? Do you? What about racism; where do you stand on that? If I was lesbian or gay, could I be a Hare Krishna devotee?

The world we live in may look like it's in a state of dysfunction. More often than not, we are faced with situations that pose challenging questions to our spiritual practice. For a spiritual practitioner, it is imperative to be conversant with the philosophy and practice of Krishna consciousness in order to effectively deal with difficult circumstances. Even though the books that explain the philosophy may have been written centuries ago, the knowledge therein is applicable to all situations even now; it just depends on the correct judgement on the spiritualist's part.

Is the Gita a book of peace or violence?

Neither. It is the record of an enlightening, hour-long conversation between Krishna and His warrior friend Arjuna on the battlefield. Krishna urges His friend to fight the upcoming battle, reasoning that it is a legitimate fight and that it is his duty as a soldier to do so. But the inner revelation of the Bhagavad Gita is that whatever one does, if it is done purely for the satisfaction of God and at His request, then the actions taken are free from any question of immorality. Neither self-serving peace nor selfish violence are the subjects of the Gita.

Isn't it better to help people instead of practising religion?

Helping others is important and is the duty of all human beings. For many different reasons, people suffer—poverty, abuse, war and disease. And it is in everyone's interest to help wherever possible. Helping others relieves suffering, develops our compassion and contributes to a peaceful society. It also helps in deciding our destination after this life ends. A life devoted to helping others means that we will be reborn in fortunate circumstances or even attain heaven.

Unfortunately, any promotion to the heavenly regions or birth in a fortunate family in the next life is only temporary. Sadly, the relief of suffering we can provide in this world is also temporary. The soul is eternal, and only when we become reunited with God in the eternal abode, will we or anyone else be free from suffering. Devotional service to Krishna is, therefore, the all-encompassing activity that will result in helping people in all conditions, in this life and the next.

In Hare Krishna, do the men look down on women?

Not at all. In fact, the Vedic scriptures are very direct in describing how women are to be respected by men, especially by men on a spiritual path. The following is taken from the Lakshmi Tantra, chapter 43. The goddess Lakshmi is speaking:

> A man of piety, free from sin, consistently adhering to the precepts of the sacred scriptures, performs those deeds that are not condemned by women and that please them.
>
> A yogi should never abuse a woman, either in deed, speech or thought. He who abuses women abuses me, He who abuses me abuses the entire three worlds. Knowing women as my direct manifestation, how can a yogi refrain from revering them?
>
> One should never hurt women, and should never even think of wronging women. A yogi who wishes to attain the fulfilment of yoga should always act to please women. He should regard all women as mothers, as goddesses, as my very self.

Why does God allow evil?

For the same reason that He allows gravity. The natural force of gravity is neither good nor bad, but you must understand it and be respectful of it, otherwise it can harm you. There are invisible laws of nature that must also be understood in order to protect ourselves from present and future harm.

Just as a child may not know the rules of driving on the road but may learn them as they grow up, we must enquire what the rules of 'driving' our own biological vehicle, the human body, are. There are good and bad deeds, and the reactions to these will come to us in the life after this one.

Just as there is a consequence when we throw a stone high in the air, there is a result for every action we throw out into this world. We need to learn the laws and obey them. When we disobey God's laws and act against them, that is the path to greater evil. Just as we immediately see a shadow when we turn away from the sun, we immediately see darkness and may commit evil actions when we turn away from God.

Is blood donation okay? What do you say about organ donation?

Yes. Blood donation is a great act of charity that may allow someone else to heal, or to survive an accident or operation. Organ donation is in the same category.

Since we do not believe in the resurrection of the body, our beliefs do not require that the entire body be buried as in the Abrahamic faiths. Therefore, the arrangement of donating one's organs after death is a final act of charity enabling someone else's life to be enhanced.

Am I responsible for bad karma if they commit sins with my organs?

No. No more than you would be charged with burglary if a burglar stole your car and used it one night.

Can I have medicines that come in alcohol or gelatine capsules?

There are often medicines available that do not come in a tincture of alcohol. It is best to use those if you can. Although when you are using alcohol for medicinal use, there can always be room for unscrupulous use at some stage. It does happen. Regarding gelatine capsules, these are directly made from the results of animal slaughter, so it is best to avoid them if you can. There are many vegetarian capsules that can be taken as an alternative. Try always to find the ahimsa or non-violent alternative if you can. If it is not available, the more people ask, the more manufacturers will respond to customer demands. That's the way the market works.

Are leather and animal products okay if I'm a vegetarian?

Not really. They are the products of extreme violence, mainly towards cows, and if you can avoid them, please do so. Leather shoes and leather sofas are the two most common items found in the homes of otherwise strict Hindu vegetarians. There are always alternatives if we look a little harder and try to avoid the hidden violence in everything we buy. We don't eat beef, and we call the cow our mother, so why do we wear her skin on our feet and sit on her skin in our homes? It is not logical or free from karmic reaction.

What do you think of racism?

Our philosophy teaches that there are numberless souls, each unique but spiritually identical. Each soul lives inside a body with different characteristics. Like passengers seated inside different vehicles. Just as some of us have small or large cars, trucks or vans, coloured ones or metallic ones, new models or old bangers, English, German or Japanese ones, we also have biological vehicles or different bodies. If someone forgets they are the driver of a car and instead starts thinking they are that car and telling friends: 'You know, I'm actually a Honda,' their friends will think they'd temporarily lost touch with reality.

So our body is simply a vehicle, and the soul is the passenger. We need to think, 'I am an eternal soul, and this body I'm in is temporary'. Thinking of oneself as belonging to a particular ethnicity, tribe or nationality is therefore an unhelpful designation. Either it is falsely imposed by others or we impose it on ourselves. Whatever the situation, it is a case of wrongful labelling. Racism is where this mistaken identity is further compounded by negative discrimination directed towards someone because of those external labels. It produces only tension and conflict.

What are your views on homosexuality?

Sexual orientation is another artificial designation of the soul. Each soul is born into the world with a stock of karma from the last life, and will enjoy a variety of happiness and distress accordingly. Some are born with ambivalent gender, and some experience passions for those of the same sex. Both of these are considered karmic complications that may make life harder for that individual. Homosexuality is not a new phenomenon—thousands of years ago, the Vedic culture named homosexuals *tritiya prakriti*, or 'the third sex'. According to the Vedas, it is not a major issue, merely a phenomenon that must be dealt with by the respective individuals. The difficulty for homosexuals in modern society is that they have been first persecuted and criminalized, then pushed forward for special treatment as fashionable victims. Neither approach is recommended by the Vedas. Homosexuals are to be treated with the respect and understanding afforded to everyone else.

14

Spirit + Ritual

Spiritual life is about internal development, a change in consciousness from matter to spirit. But the path of Krishna consciousness seems to involve a number of ritualized actions that appear to be external. One may question the need for ritualistic actions in everyday life and their relevance to one's inner development. The truth of the matter is that although our external actions may not always be internally inspired, they nevertheless produce helpful adjustments of consciousness.

What do I do if I find chanting boring?

According to psychologists, there are several reasons for boredom. One is when you have lots of mental energy and there are many things you'd *like* to be doing but you can't because you *have* to do something else. This can also result in you feeling you're not in control of the situation, and that you've somehow been forced to be there. Boredom also comes from an inability to focus your mind on the activity you've chosen to do. There's another soundtrack playing in the back of your mind and you can't concentrate.

For all these situations, here are some tips:

(1) Remind yourself that the chanting is your personal commitment—something you decided to do because you knew it would make you happier, and not because someone else asked you. Know that you're working towards a future goal of a new, improved you.

(2) Understand that at the beginning of your meditation period, there will usually be some mental resistance.

It normally takes some minutes before your roaming mind settles down and relaxes into the rhythm of the mantra. Don't give up before this happens.

(3) Minimize mental distractions by not eating late at night. Overnight digestion produces dreams that affect the mind the next morning. Spicy food also produces a restless 'morning-after' mind and disturbs concentration.

(4) Try doing your meditation at the most advantageous time of the day, before the *raja-guna* begins around 8 a.m. Before sunrise is the best time. Give up a little sleep if you have to.

(5) Don't use your mind to make decisions or think of anything stressful just before you begin meditating—and don't deviate into anything else during meditation.

How can I better understand the books and philosophy?

A book is a written conversation, and as such, it often needs more conversation to bring out the full meaning. Every sacred text usually comes with a *bhasya*, a commentary, and that also has an explanation known as a *tika* or *tipani*. You get the idea. The process is that the sacred conversation is made increasingly relevant and personal as it is expanded by qualified discussion. The ultimate point of this is when you sit with a guru, and he or she makes it all relevant to you. The principle is that you need to find someone who knows more about the text, put your questions to them, reveal your challenges and doubts, and listen carefully.

You seem to have gone from purely spiritual to ritual—why all the rituals?

There is a common misconception that rituals are man-made—a set of behaviours artificially stuck onto something purely spiritual and 'ritual-free'. The facts of the matter are quite different. Ritual has always been a part of the spiritual path, since the very beginning. The Vedic Pancharatra texts describe ceremonial temple or home worship of the very same Vishnu mentioned in the Rig Veda, while the Yajur Veda describes elaborate fire ceremonies. Rituals such as these are an external manifestation of an evolved consciousness. If we perform the same rituals, our consciousness will also evolve. Therefore, they are not to be dispensed with as being superfluous to spiritual life—they are an intrinsic and time-tested element of it.

Why are coconuts and bananas used so much in ceremonies?

In Vedic science, there is a hierarchy of plant life—poisonous or other harmful plants are considered to be at the bottom, and the most beneficial, useful and delicious plants are at the top. Coconuts and bananas are right at the top. They grow in abundance, have health-giving properties and can be used for a multitude of purposes. They are the gifts of God to humans and hence, are offered back to Him in ceremonies.

What's a fire sacrifice all about?

It's another way of making offerings to God. Fire is a natural element. Half of it is visible and half invisible, representing the transition between the world we can see with our eyes and the world we can't. The grains and ghee we offer into the flames are transformed by fire and transferred to the world we cannot see. More than this though, it is a way of actually connecting to gods or God through the act of yagya. Traditionally, it was the primary way of making offerings, later supplanted by temple worship and most recently, by the recitation of the names of God—the sacrifice of the names, or *Nama Yagya*. But we still preserve the fire ceremonies for life-cycle events and important occasions.

Aside from weddings, what other religious ceremonies are there?

There are customs and ceremonies for each important stage of life. These are known as *samskaras*. Different numbers of ceremonies are given by various authors, but the main ones are ten in number and are as follows: the wedding (*vivaha*), conception (*garbhadana*), the birth ceremony (*jata*), the first visit to the temple (*nishkramanam*), the naming ceremony (*nama karana*), the giving of the first grain food (*anna prasana*), haircutting (*chuda karana*) and the first day of school (*vidya-rambha*). Before the age of sixteen comes the vedic initiation (*upanayanam*) followed by, once again, the wedding! At the end of life, there are the funeral rites (*antyesti*). All these ceremonies can be conducted by a brahman, and make enjoyable and memorable life celebrations.

Why do we put our two hands together in a gesture of 'Namaste'?

The universal greeting of placing the two palms together before the heart is a gesture of respect for others, saints, gods and God. Gestures like these are an embodiment of an inner thought—just making the gesture helps to create the inner thought. It is one of the aspects of the science of ritual. The word 'namaste', as many already know, means 'I offer my respects to you', and can be witnessed everywhere. The gesture can also be given as a hello, goodbye or thank you.

Why do the devotees at the temple say 'Jaya!' and raise both their hands?

This is a gesture of exultation or happy celebration. When we feel that something great has been achieved, we raise both arms and cheer. This is a universal gesture, whether in sports, music or at times of great joy. It is also a gesture seen at a time of spiritual awakening, when all cares and anxieties have been relieved. The gesture can also be seen in the figures of the *Pancha Tattva*, the five associates who spread the teachings of Krishna 500 years ago in India. They danced and sang together, raising their arms and crying out 'Jaya!' The word *jaya* means 'Victory!'

Why do we not touch paper, books or other people with our feet?

The feet are the lowest part of our person. In a dry, hot climate, they are also unhygienic, carrying dirt and dust. The head is our highest part and is said to carry our pride. When we express our humility, we bow down, bringing our head to the lowest level. This is particularly so when we bow down at the feet of God or a person who has dedicated their life to God. While the feet of a saint are said to be the place where we can lose our pride and become elevated in spirit, our own feet are considered to be quite the opposite. If we think highly of the spiritual credentials of others, it will be a natural consequence for us to consider our own feet to be not worthy of anyone else's bowing. In this way, and out of respect, we do not touch anyone else with our feet, neither any holy article nor anything that is to be used in service to God.

What is the ceremony with the waving of a peacock fan?

Arati means 'to greet', and is a festive ritual held six times every day. The service is a ceremonial presentation of a series of articles offered to the Lord on the altar. Such pleasing items as incense, lamps, flowers, fresh water, cloth and cooling fans—including one made of a Tibetan yak's tail and another of peacock feathers—are waved before the deity to the accompaniment of the blowing of a conch shell, the ringing of a bell and the chanting of prescribed mantras. The public can come witness this and receive blessings in the form of sanctified items as they are passed out from the altar. All the while, the congregation join in singing the kirtan being led with cymbals and drums.

I saw some special plants in the greenhouse—what are they?

They are tulasi plants, also known by the Latin names of *Ocimum tenuiflorum* and *Ocimum sanctum*. Tulasi is sacred to all those who worship Vishnu or Krishna. Every time a plate of food is offered on the altar, a leaf of the tulasi plant is placed on the top. Garlands made of fresh, leafy tulasi sprigs are offered to the deity, and the buds and flowers of the plant are placed upon His feet.

The devotees wear two or three strands of small wooden beads on their necks that are made of the tulasi stems. The devotee's meditation beads, or japa-mala, are also often made of wood from the tulasi bush.

You'll see a plant or two decorating the altar—every morning, one of these plants is offered a short arati ceremony while devotees sing a special song describing the benefits of worshipping the tulasi plant. Because tulasi grows best in a tropical climate, the greenhouses are always kept warm.

What does the OM symbol mean?

It's not actually a symbol, although it is often used in that way as a generic indicator of Hinduism. OM, or AUM is actually a word made up of three letters of the Sanskrit alphabet. It is a kind of respectful address, or invocation, and is the first word in the many verses of the Vedas, the sacred scriptures of the tradition.

Occasionally, I've even seen a swastika used in temples—I thought that was a Nazi symbol?

Actually, it's an ancient symbol of good fortune. The very word *swastika* means 'May good luck be here'. It was used all over the ancient world in slightly different forms, including in Britain. Before the rise of the National Socialist Party in Germany, the symbol was very common on greeting cards and lucky charms. Unfortunately, it was misappropriated, and now no one can see it these days without thinking of the terrors of the Second World War.

15

At the Temple

The term for a temple in ancient Sanskrit is 'mandir', which literally means 'where the mind becomes steady'. Although one's inner state of consciousness is the most important factor in one's spiritual life, the temple with all its rituals and regulated ceremonies has a lot to do with achieving that state of consciousness. Understanding why we do what we do can add a lot of value to the activities we carry out at the temple, and thus accelerate our spiritual progress.

Why do I need to come to the temple? God is everywhere.

Yes, that's true, but it is not always easy to see Him everywhere. For this reason, it is helpful to go to a place set aside for that purpose. Many people find the forests, beaches or mountains helpful for thinking of God because those places are relatively free from distraction. But the image of God manifesting on the altar is an important part of focusing your mind on Him, and according to the Pancharatra texts, God actually appears directly in His temple image. So you can directly perform sacred services to Him in that spot. The other benefits of coming to the temple are that you get the experience of shared worship—something unavailable by yourself. You get to enjoy the company of like-minded people, and also have enlightening conversations and delicious blessed food afterwards.

Why do I have to learn Sanskrit prayers? Why can't I pray in my own language?

God understands every language spoken on Earth, including the voices of all the animals, so you don't have to speak to Him in a special language during your prayer. But if you'd like to share in the hymns and songs spoken and sung by the greatest of His saints, as well as learn the words actually spoken by Him during His avatars, that opportunity is available to you.

Besides, Sanskrit is a beautiful-sounding language, and the poetry composed by the great devotees is particularly pleasing. (The translations into native languages are also available so that you can know what you are saying.) These days, Sanskrit verses and expressions are a common way of communicating with devotees of Krishna all over the world. There is also a revival of Sanskrit right now—it is spoken as a living language by around 2,00,000 people.

Why do you have to give money? Is that part of the tradition?

You don't have to do anything that makes you feel uncomfortable, but if you feel grateful for what you've received at the temple, or if you'd like to support the good work carried out by the devotees, then a contribution is always welcome. The temple runs on the kindness of our supporters, and we'd like to think that Krishna blesses those who give according to their means.

Money is simply an easy way to give a small proportion of your day's work, but you can also come and volunteer your time and skills to the cause of Krishna's service. Certainly, it is a part of the tradition to give something to support the worship and the mission to reach out to others.

When there is a death in the family, why can I not come to the temple?

Mourning for a loved one, and the extra observations involved with a death and preparing for a funeral, all take time. According to tradition, during this period, it is also considered proper that one restricts one's socializing or going out. Instead, relatives and friends visit the home. The temple also visits the home in the form of the devotees who sing the names of Krishna and read out loud sacred books, such as the Bhagavad Gita. According to one's family tradition, the period may last from a few days up to one month. It is also customary that no cooking is done in the home. Instead, friends take turns to cook simple dishes—at least for a few days. The mourners cannot serve food to those who visit their homes and visitors cannot eat in the home until the mourning period is over.

What happens at a Hare Krishna funeral?

A funeral has several purposes. It is a chance for mourners to come and express their own grief and offer condolences to the family and friends of the departed. It is also an opportunity to give thanks for the life of the person who has died, and to recount some of their contributions and what a difference they made in the lives of others. Since it is the very last stage of the soul's embodied journey for this life, prayers are said for the continued journey of the departed towards Krishna. Finally, it is a time to say goodbye and commit the mortal remains back to the elements. In our funerals, that element is fire. Sometimes, the mourners will line up to scatter flower petals into the open coffin. Hare Krishna funerals take place in modern crematoria and usually last forty minutes. The ashes of the deceased are often taken to India for ceremonial dispersal in a holy river.

Why do we walk in a circle around something?

This is a ritual or ceremonial act of respect for a holy person or object that is not limited to India or Hinduism. It is known as *pradakshina* or circumambulation. It is performed in a clockwise direction, often by walking in three circles. It is said that to walk in this way, keeping the right shoulder towards the holy centre serves to bind the holiness to your heart. The opposite is to walk in the anti-clockwise direction, known as *apradakshina*, which serves to distance the holiness from the heart. When Ravana was on the battlefield with Sri Rama, he circled around Him in this way.

Why do we regard trees and plants as sacred?

All life is sacred, even trees and plants. To cut a tree with no purpose is considered a sin. But sometimes, if a particular tree is *swasti*, or auspicious, or if the plant gives us life, shade or blessings, we offer respects to it, considering it as a gift from God. In this way, even a common plant or tree may serve to remind us of God and His many blessings. In some rare cases, the plant is the earthly manifestation of a higher, divine personality. Such is the case with the plant known as tulasi. In the higher realms, she is a divine female attendant of Sri Krishna. Her leaves are picked and placed upon every food offering taken to the shrine. Each morning, the devotees assemble to sing a song dedicated to her and to walk around her in respect. To water her is considered to be an act of devotion to Krishna. After she dies, her wood is taken to make the neck beads (*kanthimala*) that devotees wear, as well as the meditation beads (japa-mala).

What is the significance of the lotus? Why do we say 'lotus eyes' and so on?

Viewed from any angle or at any stage of its growth, the lotus flower is the most beautiful of all flowers. While nothing in this world can actually compare to its divine creator, this has not prevented poets from comparing the Lord's form to the most beautiful wonders of the natural world. Krishna's face has thus been compared to a fully bloomed lotus in its radiance, and His eyes are compared to the shape of the lotus petal. The palms of His hands and feet are compared to the pink lotus and His bodily colour to the beauty of a blue lotus. The gradually expanding consciousness of the devotee is compared to the slowly blooming lotus.

Why do we blow the conch?

The conch is one of nature's musical instruments. When the end of the empty shell is cut and the air is blown through the inner coils, it sounds like a sonorous trumpet. The deep and resonant note produced is also said to resemble the sound of OM. It attracts the attention of all who hear it, even from a distance—especially when more than one is blown at the same time. It can be seen in the hands of Vishnu and Sri Krishna; Arjuna and all the warriors blew their respective conches to herald their presence before the great battle of Kurukshetra. The conch, or *shanka*, is blown at the beginning and end of every arati ceremony, and on special or ceremonial occasions.

Why are women and men separated in the temple?

That is a custom to help preserve the one-pointed spiritual focus of the temple. It helps to maintain the sanctity of the space, and the natural tendency to socialize before the altar is kept in check. Besides, sometimes the temple is extremely crowded and a little separation serves to protect women from being pushed. But it's just in the temple room itself and other crowded spaces—there is no separation anywhere else.

What is the significance of flowers being passed from the altar?

All items that are first offered to Krishna on the altar are afterwards offered to everyone else. The item is then considered to be 'non-different' from Krishna and a blessing to be received by the grateful devotees. The flowers can be smelled, as can the aroma of fragrant incense, and the delicious food offerings can be tasted. There is great pleasure in accepting these items that have been offered to Krishna that are known as *prasada*, or 'mercy', and accepted as a great blessing.

Why is the flame of a lamp touched?

This heat and light of the lamp flame is also prasada, having been offered in veneration to the Lord. The ceremony is known as arati and is a part of the ceremonial worship known as puja. The word 'arati' comes from the Sanskrit *aratrika*, which means 'that which removes darkness'. The flame is simply touched with the fingers and the heat is applied to the head. Some worshippers like to think of the flame as a protection, or that when the flame's heat is transferred to their eyes, they will perhaps begin to develop the inner vision to see the Lord as He is.

Why do we show our left side when bowing?

It is a tradition to show the right shoulder to a holy person when walking around them, and the left shoulder when bowing down. Service is always performed from the right-hand side of the person you are serving, which means you will stand to the left as seen by others. Consequently, the services are offered from the left of the altar, where the priest stands.

Why do people bow down to each other or touch their feet?

It is said that 'freedom from pride opens the gate to the eternal realm', and so the cultivation of humility is important for those on the path of Bhakti yoga. Humility is a voluntary acceptance of the worth of another and is brought about by spiritual cultivation. It has nothing to do with humiliation, which is a negative emotional state. Offering our respect, gratitude and service to others helps foster our humility while bowing down immediately diminishes our pride. It is quite common throughout the Eastern world to bow to elders and teachers, and in India, touching the feet is another way of offering respect. However, touching the feet is usually done with the permission of the other person, and mostly when that person is already one's teacher, guide or elder relative.

Why do we take our shoes off before entering the temple? And why can't we wear slippers?

The temple is a clean and sanctified space, and shoes always tend to bring in the dirt from outside. Removing the shoes (and taking off one's hat or covering one's head) are also ways of indicating that you're coming into the presence of someone greater than yourself. Traditionally, shoes are left in a special room for that purpose. You may wear slippers inside the temple building, but not in the temple room itself. The only exception made is for the disabled.

Do you have priests?

We would define a priest as someone who conducts religious services on behalf of others. In the temple, we have a system of training and initiation so that over four years, a member can become qualified to conduct religious services. The priests serve on the altar and can be seen on the main shrine performing the arati ceremony. They also conduct life-passage services such as birth ceremonies, weddings and funerals. We consider the priest to be a role and not a spiritual level—a person's devotion is the real measure of their spirituality, not their ceremonial function. Both men and women serve as priests.

Why is there a bell just inside the temple room door?

You are entering the Lord's private chamber, so to draw attention to your entrance and indicate that you are here only for service, you lightly ring the bell. Not loudly, just enough for Him to hear—and He has very acute ears! You have come for an audience (*darshan*) with God, so you can go immediately to the shrine, bow down and make your prayers. Taking photographs is not an immediate priority. Imagine you were with a very important person—you would probably speak with them before taking a picture! So it is with Krishna. The etiquette observed is not to talk in front of the altar and not to eat anything directly in front.

What are the curtains on the shrine for, and why can't we have darshan at all times?

The curtains are closed during the times when the deities are being bathed and dressed when meals are served to Them, and while They are resting. To avoid disappointment, you can learn the times of darshan and arati services, six of which are held throughout the day, from 4.30 a.m. through to 9 p.m. There is always enough time to see the deities if you plan ahead.

Is all the food at the temple cooked by the devotees?

Yes, the cooking of food six times a day is an important part of the worship of Krishna. We have two kitchens; one is described as the 'deity kitchen', and all the food cooked there is only for the altar offerings. When an offering is cooked, it is placed on silver dishes—one for each deity—and is known as *naivedyam*. After the offerings have been made, there is a long period while the Lord eats, after which the food is known as *prasadam*. It is not only delicious but full of blessings. Devotees are ecstatic to be served even a small portion of it.

Why do some Vaishnava temples have a painting of Vishnu with a lion's face?

That is Narasimha or Nrsimhadeva, the half-man, half-lion form of Vishnu. When the demon king Hiranyakashipu persecuted his saintly son Prahlada, it was more than the Lord could bear. He burst out of a pillar to battle with the king, eventually dispatching him upon His knees. Although the image looks somewhat grisly, the devotees like it because it reminds them that no matter where they are, the Lord will always protect them.

What is the painting of the five people with their hands in the air?

Those five figures are collectively known as the pancha-tattva, or 'the absolute truth in five features'. Krishna comes into this world as His own devotee, and accompanied by these four associates, travels and spreads the religious practice for the age by chanting the names of God. Depicted from left to right, you will see Advaita-Acharya, Nityananda Prabhu, Chaitanya Mahaprabhu, Gadadhara Pandit and Srivasa Thakur. They have their hands up because they are dancing together in *sankirtan*, the group chanting of the Hare Krishna mantra.

Why do people bow down?

It is said that the head carries our pride, and by lowering the head before God, we rise in humility. All religions practise some form of bending, kneeling or bowing before the altar. The version you'll see in the temple will be one of getting down on both knees and placing the hands in front of you, then touching the floor with your head. The other form is lying face down on the floor with legs and arms outstretched. This is known as 'becoming like a stick' or *dandavat*.

Do I have to sit cross-legged in the temple?

We can provide a chair if you need one. We know that everyone's knees can't always manage sitting cross-legged for more than a few minutes. But it does slightly slow the blood flow to the lower body, and consequently, there's more blood that gets to the brain. All the better for your thinking about spiritual things! That posture is traditional, and some find it helpful, but if being comfortable is more important, any posture is good—apart from falling asleep!

What are the yellow scarves with red writing on them?

Those are cotton shawls with the Sanskrit words of the Hare Krishna mantra printed on them. They can help to keep you warm. Devotees use them at times of prayer or ceremony, or at any other time to show the 'team' they support! They are only intended for the upper body, however, and must never be used to wrap the legs since they have the divine names of God printed on them.

What is the white liquid in a silver bowl by the altar?

Krishna is bathed in the morning with yogurt, honey and tulasi buds. Some of this is collected as it flows down to His feet and transferred to a bowl where three drops are taken in their right hands by temple visitors. This is a very special blessing and is said to prevent untimely death. The drink is known as 'the nectar of the feet' or *charana-amrita*.

What is the Gayatri?

The Gayatri is the name given to a poetic metre of twenty-four syllables. There are many Gayatri mantras, but the term is most commonly used to indicate a particular mantra known as the Brahma Gayatri—the mantra given at the time of *upanayanam*, the initiation (*diksha*) ceremony. This mantra is accompanied by investiture with the sacred thread, given to young males, often between the ages of eight and sixteen. The Brahma Gayatri was originally given by Lord Krishna to Brahma, who was then inspired to speak the Veda. It is a secret mantra given by the guru to the disciple and is not meant to be broadcasted as, for instance, in the form of singing it loudly.

16

Regulated Devotion

Along with the rituals, the path of Krishna consciousness seems to place a great emphasis on counting things: there are numbers for rounds of japa and regulative principles, and lists for almost everything else. There are also many other rules. How important are lists and rules, and why?

If Krishna's name is not different from Him, why do I not feel anything while chanting?

Perhaps you are distracted by other thoughts. Even the thought of 'I'm not feeling anything' is a serious distraction. The chanting works if you both chant and listen attentively, allowing the mantra to supersede any other thoughts you might be having. Even if your mind drifts away from the chanting, simply bring it back and refocus. You'll experience something if you chant for long enough.

Why do I have to chant a fixed number of rounds?

It takes around a month to develop a new habit, and new habits are best developed by daily regulation. Counting the number of times you go around the circle of 108 japa beads is a traditional practice—it fixes your mind during a set period of chanting, prevents you from chanting less than your chosen commitment and provides you with a sense of achievement.

Can you chant without beads?

Yes, you can chant without beads, but you'll find it impossible to count how many times you've chanted without using them! Devotees have traditionally used a string of beads made of carved wood, often from the medicinal neem tree or the sacred tulasi. Should one not have access to japa beads, it is possible to use the thumb to count the twelve finger joints nine times (108) or to use a tally counter.

Why can't you do it privately?

Mantra meditation is a private practice in the sense that it is your contemplation and doesn't involve anyone else. But if you chant with others, there is the benefit of mutual support and concentration.

Why do people have bags on their hands? Why are people pointing when they're chanting?

The bags are used because it is customary not to display the japa beads while chanting on them. They are also used to keep the beads clean, and the strap can be used to hang the bag around the neck. The finger 'pointing' out of the bead bag is not actually pointing at anything at all. The index finger is known as *ahamkara,* or the ego finger and is used to accuse others when the ego is aroused. As a consequence, it is traditionally kept away from sacred items such as beads or other ritual objects.

Do I have to chant every day?

Do you brush your teeth every day? Do you eat every day? Do you sleep every night? If the answer is yes, it will be because what you do every day is very important. We tend to do less important tasks less frequently. But we perform the most important tasks every day. Our life depends on what we do every day. Chanting the maha-mantra is the most important thing that anyone can do because it frees the soul, and that is the very purpose of life. Like eating, chanting nourishes us; like brushing our teeth, chanting cleans our mind; and like sleeping, chanting restores our vitality. So yes, chant every day!

Is it better to chant one round well rather than more rounds in a distracted way?

This is a question that does not have an either/or answer. Both are important. It is very good to chant one round well, free from offensive mentality or distraction. But if you did chant such a round, you would immediately chant some more—you wouldn't be able to resist it! In order to reach the stage of chanting one pure round, you'd have to have already gone through the stage of chanting many more rounds in a distracted way. The first round comes with distraction, and then comes the one round without it. The first is probable and the second is entirely possible. Both are important, but one focused round of japa is better, so aim for that, then chant more of them!

Is it more important to chant or to read?

They are both important. From the chanting, we develop the desire to read the scriptures daily, and from the scriptures, we'll understand how important the chanting is. But they do have relative importance. An example: water and oxygen are both important for our lives. We can survive without water for seven days, but without oxygen, we can survive for only seven minutes. They are both essential for our survival, but one depends on the other—without oxygen, you can't drink water. Similarly, without chanting you can't do anything else. Chanting is the one essential practice upon which all the other aspects of spiritual life depend.

Is japa more important than kirtan?

Kirtan is easier for those who are newcomers to the maha-mantra—there is the melody, the musical accompaniment, the rhythm, the companionship, the call-and-response singing, the elevated, joyful mood in the room and the dancing. All of this makes an attractive environment in which to experience Krishna's holy names. Japa by comparison is a relatively lonely pursuit, involving only one tongue, two ears and some wooden beads. And yet, the sound of the maha-mantra is the same in both cases. The difference with japa is that in just seven minutes, we can chant one attentive round of 108 mantras. The same number of mantras in musical kirtan mode would take at least thirty-six minutes. To sing sixteen rounds worth of maha-mantras—1728 mantras—would take over nine hours. So for sheer practicality and sustainability in our daily life, it seems more advisable to make your japa the foundation of everything.

Why are sixteen rounds the standard?

Sixteen rounds are the standard for initiation, but many devotees have made their decision to chant more or fewer rounds than this. Some chant four rounds, for instance, and treat it as their standard. Others chant six, eight, twelve, twenty, twenty-five or thirty-two as a standard. What is important is to choose your standard and stick with it. The number can be increased gradually. In India, sixty-four rounds each day is a standard for many devotees, but when Srila Prabhupada tried to introduce this in 1966, his young followers protested. When even thirty-two was too much, he finally drew the line and so sixteen rounds became the standard for his initiated disciples. To become a disciple today simply means to follow this original request, and to not go below that number. However, Srila Prabhupada felt that he was being particularly lenient and mentioned that this full complement of rounds could be completed in less than two hours. 'You have twenty-four hours,' he reasoned with his disciples. He felt that ninety minutes or two hours wasn't too much of an imposition on them. Additionally, when the mantra meditation is done properly, the experience of chanting is so pleasurable that time simply flies by.

What is Ekadasi?

Ekadasi means the eleventh day of the moon and occurs twice in a month. Just as certain places have a special atmosphere conducive to our purification and spiritual advancement, so do certain phases of time. The Ekadasi day is spiritually surcharged with devotional energy. On this day, we do not eat grains, beans, legumes or anything containing them. There are many side benefits from observing Ekadasi, such as good health (regular fasting allows our digestive organs to rest) and economy (if everyone followed Ekadasi, imagine how much food would be saved). But by far the main purpose of following Ekadasi is to help us awaken our love for Krishna. Srila Prabhupada taught that following Ekadasi means minimizing the demands of the body and maximizing our service to Krishna. On Ekadasi, we should eat more simply and try to put into practice the maxim: 'Eat to live, not live to eat'. He advised that on Ekadasi, we increase our chanting of the holy names. To a disciple who asked, 'Should we chant twenty-five rounds on Ekadasi?' Srila Prabhupada replied, 'Why only twenty-five rounds? You should chant as many as possible.'

17

Outreach

There's probably nothing the world likes less right now than a religious preacher. Either a figure of fun or a threatening source of volatile rhetoric, the preacher is almost universally mistrusted. And yet, the Krishna consciousness movement is a 'preaching mission'. So what about preaching for Krishna? Is it still relevant or appropriate today to try to change people's minds about belief? Here, we look at the difference between sharing a message and conversion, and overcoming our resistance once we've decided to share Krishna's teachings with others.

Why do you sing in public places? Isn't religion a private thing?

Your relationship with God and your prayers to Him are definitely private. But if God Himself appeared before you and asked you to sing His names so that others could hear, what would you do? In the Srimad Bhagavatam, compiled 5000 years ago, it was predicted that a golden incarnation would appear in the Age of Kali, the present age, and that He would sing the names of Krishna surrounded by His associates. When Krishna appeared in this form, that is exactly what He did and asked everyone else to do.* That congregational singing, or *Harinama-sankirtan*, was spread all over India, and has carried on until the present day. Now, you will see people of all nations, in every major city of the world, singing the Hare Krishna mantra with drums and cymbals. It gives millions of people the chance to hear the transcendental names of Krishna and continue their spiritual journey with fresh inspiration.

I believe that knowledge should be free. Why do you ask for money for your books?

Knowledge is free, but book production is costly, so we ask everyone for a small contribution to help

* Srimad Bhagavatam 11.5.32 ('In the Age of Kali, intelligent persons perform congregational chanting to worship the incarnation of Godhead who constantly sings the names of Krishna.')

with the printing. In our temples, there are two or three daily classes that are free to all visitors—every day of the week, throughout the year. Similarly, we distribute large quantities of delicious prasadam for free to all comers. Bookselling is one way we support everything else we do. Our books are printed in large quantities, sometimes 1 lakh for just one title, which keeps the costs down. We also give them away if people genuinely have no money. No one is denied. But if someone can make a donation to cover the cost or even a little more to support the temple, they will have an interesting book at much less than it would cost in a shop, and they will have done a good deed by supporting charitable work.

Aren't you worried about all the attention you get when you sing outside?

Singing with cymbals and Indian drums in public is not a form of exhibitionism, entertainment or selfish attention-seeking. The chanting of the names of God in call-and-response fashion is an act of sharing the practice with others, giving them an opportunity to experience it for themselves and perhaps try it out when they get home. There are many devotees today who had their first experience of Krishna consciousness through street singing. Practically speaking, that is where it all began, with Srila Prabhupada singing under a tree in a park in New York City. The vision of devotees singing in the street is the enduring image of Hare Krishna all around the world.

Why are you trying to convert people?

Krishna consciousness does not involve a 'conversion' from one religion to another. It is not a set of religious beliefs amongst many others. The path of Bhakti yoga is a spiritual discipline that can easily restore our dormant relationship with God, no matter how we may worship Him presently, or which holy book we honour. God is not Christian, Muslim, Jewish or Hindu. The soul is also none of these—it is purely spiritual by nature but has forgotten God. Bhakti yoga is non-sectarian and universal. It consists simply of serving God without any selfish motive. If a person is a Christian or Muslim, we ask them not to convert but to add something to their life—the practices of bhakti.

Aren't we destined to practice a certain religion? Why are you trying to change that?

You might have been born into a family or community that practised its faith in a particular way. That much was your destiny. But you are also born with the free will to enquire and discover how to further your spiritual progress in this life. That's something different from having a religious badge. Faith in God is not about the culture of your birth community; it's the deepest part of you. The part of you that needs to find answers. Krishna consciousness is the original consciousness of the soul, not a set of sectarian religious beliefs. You have an identity that you're born with, and as you pass through life, you adopt many other identities, most of which you can decide to change. You can change your hairstyle, the way you dress, your name, your nationality, your educational qualifications and your career. Similarly, you can also change your religion. All of them are external to the real you and none mean that you become a different person. That part of you doesn't change—the real you always remain the same. Krishna consciousness is therefore not about changing religion—it's about growing your spirituality within, whatever religion you follow.

But you do ask everyone to read the Bhagavad Gita, don't you? That sounds like proselytizing to me.

Most people don't like the idea of aggressively arguing for a set of beliefs. Such behaviour alienates others, causes disturbance and is hardly ever successful. But imagine you've just seen a good movie. You enjoyed it and found the story uplifting. Now you want to urge all your friends to see it too. Is that proselytizing or preaching? Yes, by definition, it may be. The word 'preach' means 'to exhort a person to a higher level of action', something that will make them healthier or happier. In this case, persuading them to go to the cinema. In the same way, if the teachings of the Bhagavad Gita have made you one degree happier, then telling others about it is the greatest service you could do for them.

If making others happy by sharing something I enjoy is 'preaching', then I can be a preacher. But how can I overcome my fear of speaking to others?

Most of us have two main fears regarding preaching, and the first is always this: 'What if they don't like what I'm saying and reject me?' Rejection hurts. Nobody wants to be rejected. We all want to be loved, and when we finally pluck up the courage to speak about Krishna and someone rejects our best attempts, we can't help but take it personally. The best antidote for this fear of rejection is to realize that it's not about you at all. It's only about that person and Krishna. You are merely the messenger, the postman. What they do with the message is up to them and Krishna within their heart.

And how you feel about preaching on behalf of Krishna is between you and Him. The only thing you have to do is stop wanting to be loved when you go out to preach! Just take it for granted that only one out of many people will be remotely interested, and then you'll never be disappointed. Srila Prabhupada said, 'As soon as you try to sell a diamond, you cannot expect many customers. Nonetheless, a diamond is a diamond, even if there are no customers.'*

What if I don't have enough knowledge to speak to others?

This is the second fear we have: 'I don't know enough about the Bhagavad Gita to speak about it. Besides, even if I did, I'm not convinced enough to persuade anyone else!' This kind of self-doubt is a crippling thought for the preacher. As above, it stems from the fear of rejection mixed with the self-doubt that you are insufficiently convinced.

Speaking to others about the Bhagavad Gita is a powerful method of self-purification, even if apparently unsuccessful. For instance, we might take time before to carefully consider what we'll say and rehearse our words carefully so that we don't forget what to say in the moment. But when we inevitably do forget or say the wrong thing entirely, we learn from our mistakes. On other occasions, without preparation, we speak from the heart with words that don't seem ours. At these times, we feel Krishna Himself is speaking through us, using us as an instrument. The experience

* Jon Nordheuvier, 'Young Ascetics Honor Lord Krishna', *New York Times*, 6 September 1972, https://www.nytimes.com/1972/09/06/archives/young-ascetics-honor-lord-krishna-young-members-of-ascetic-sect.html.

is so tangible that we become convinced of our actual relationship with Krishna and His affection for us.

How can I ignite interest in people? Most people don't seem to be attracted.

Yes, some people are like damp grass and others like dry grass. It takes longer for some people to reach the point of ignition! Your skill as a preacher is to say something of interest to the person in front of you, while being polite, affable, accessible and patient. Everyone finds spiritual topics marginally interesting—you just need to know what their interest is. Hence, listening is even more important than speaking. The task of a preacher is to find the spark inside someone and gently fan it into a blazing fire.

Why do we go door-to-door?

This is the original form of preaching recommended by Sri Chaitanya Mahaprabhu. In 1505 CE, Haridas Thakur and Nityananda Prabhu were the first to take the sankirtana message out to the neighbourhood in Bengal. They went *ghare-ghare* or door-to-door and were also met with a mixed response, just like our devotees today. Some things never change. Yet, from these earliest attempts, many thousands came to follow the teachings. We find that people are generally friendlier in their own homes—where the stresses of the high street or the workplace are far away, and they can offer a few minutes of their time, take a book or magazine from us, and even offer their hospitality.

Why are book distribution and Harinama so important?

As devotees, we are all assisting Srila Prabhupada in his work to share Krishna consciousness with as many as possible. Our movement has one motto: '*Jiva Doya, Nama Ruchi, Vaishnava Seva*,' which means: 'Kindness to all living beings, attraction to the divine name and service to Vaishnavas.' These are the sacred principles upon which the movement is built. Distribution of books about Krishna and the singing of the holy names of Krishna accomplish all three of these foundational principles. We have many devotees who came to Krishna as a result of a book given to them years ago. A book is a very substantial object, and once purchased, can remain on someone's bookshelf for years.

The sight of devotees singing in the streets is something unforgettable for most people. They might not join in, but they will always remember the sight and sound of the kirtan. As such, whenever they hear the Hare Krishna mantra again, they will have another opportunity to enquire more and perhaps to sing along this time.

Should we find newer and more relevant ways to spread the message?

There is actually no limit to the ways that it can be done. The only thing preventing us from doing so is our ingenuity and perseverance. Srila Prabhupada's request was that we use our intelligence and creativity to come up with new ideas to 'deliver our countrymen'. So in the 1960s, the distribution of colour magazines and large, hardbound books was done in the streets, train stations, airports and homes.

In the 1970s, the sounds of kirtan were disseminated through pop music songs and vinyl albums. The devotional theatre was developed and taken on tour in HGV trucks remodelled as temples. Films followed and in the 1980s, television and radio appearances started as well.

In the mid-1980s, the devotees of Krishna were the first to use digital broadcasting in Italy, using seventeen radio transmitters to cover the country with a twenty-four-hour Krishna Radio. A big circus tent toured the country with a festival and show.

The 1990s saw the birth of preaching Krishna consciousness through the internet. In Russia, the first Hare Krishna television studio was built.

As for relevance, Srila Prabhupada asked his disciples to speak and write 'in their own language', always making Krishna consciousness relevant and accessible by 'showing how Krishna consciousness is the solution to all the world's problems'.

18

Culture

From moustaches to cow poo and cricket, here's a miscellany of commonly-asked questions about the niggly little details of the Krishna devotee's life. Too small to ask in public but so important they won't go away, these questions are not the deepest philosophical ones, but unless you have them answered, they'll be with you forever.

Why do I have to get up early?

'Early' is a relative term—it all depends on what time you go to bed. Those who go to sleep at 8 p.m. think that 4 a.m. is the right time to get up. For this reason, the middle of the sleeping period—the middle of the night—is called 'midnight'. While people used to go to sleep and wake up earlier before, it is not so in our stressed, 24/7 world. Many are now only managing to get to sleep at midnight. Meditation the next morning is then difficult. Since the morning is actually the best time for any meditation or spiritual activity, we all need to reclaim it. In fact, if we use the morning hours, we can maximize the effect of our meditation.

What's wrong with beards or moustaches?

Nothing. You'll see that Krishna's friend Arjuna had a moustache and the great sage Vyasa had a beard. But an inordinate amount of attention on bodily looks and preening can serve to focus our attention on the externals of our life even more than we have to. Being overly consumed with appearance, fashion and bodily decoration can take much time out of our day. Added up, it totals weeks or even months of our life. Time is too precious to waste. It is better to spend any time we have remembering our eternal identity than clipping hairs in the moustache of our temporary body.

When the great sages wore beards and long hair, it was because they were ignoring their hair completely, rather than making themselves attractive.

Is astrology okay? Should I have my chart done?

Astrology or *jyotish* is a Vedic science that can help or hinder us depending on how we use it. Compared to a weather forecast, it can tell us what to expect at certain key points in our lives. It can also help in choosing a life or business partner. If we know that rain is forecast, then we can take an umbrella. Similarly, if we know that we are compatible with the personality of another, then we can form a relationship with them.

But too much dependence on astrology can be unhelpful in our dependency on Krishna and His plan for us. Although astrology is an authentic 'limb' of the Vedas, known as a *vedanga*, and offers many suggestions for a happier life, there are even higher influences to consider. According to our level of devotion, the Lord Himself takes charge of us, and because He transcends every other force of nature, His mercy causes our fate to be altered, taking us in a new direction.

What's wrong with gambling? Isn't it true that Maharaja Yudhisthira gambled?

King Yudhisthira did gamble, and as a result, he lost everything. That's the danger of gambling—you might win, but you also might lose (and you might lose a lot). That, of course, is the temptation of gambling—you have a chance of winning a fortune that you didn't work for. What could be a better proposal? We all work so hard for every penny in this world, and so much is immediately spent on living. Who would not want to win a small fortune for a small stake? Yet for a few people to win, many more gamblers have to lose. To imagine that you will be lucky, or that God has arranged for you alone to win, may be just that—your imagination. Gambling ruins lives just as much as alcohol does, and involves placing your imagination at the centre of your life rather than God, who will provide you with what you need.

What about stocks and shares?

Doing business always involves taking a risk—that risk can be said to be a form of gambling. But there is low-risk investment and extremely high-risk speculation. The greater the level of risk, the more it approaches more spiritually harmful forms of gambling. For instance, the chance of winning a national lottery might be 1 in 14 million, so that would be considered a gamble. The initial stake is lost when the gamble is lost. A bond or a share, however, may involve much less risk and can be considered proportionately less of a gamble. However, the daily meditation on the fluctuating prices of the market will take precious time away from other, less stressful pursuits.

Why can't I eat meat? I heard that Rama ate meat.

For every action, there is a reaction. When we help others, there's a good reaction—we'll enjoy it at some time in the future. When we exploit others, we'll have to experience the same level of pain they suffered. For the consumption of meat, there are several stages involved, with a commensurate level of reaction for each stage. Those who kill the animal, transport it, sell it, buy it, cook it, serve it to others and eat it, are all guilty of the killing and will have to experience the reactions to that act. Only if one is prepared to become an animal in his next life and be killed, should he eat meat. Regarding Rama, the verse which explains what He ate is in the Valmiki Ramayana, Sundarakanda, Skanda 36, Sloka 41, which says:

na mamsam raghava bhunkte
na chaiva madhu sevate
vanyam suvihitam nityam
bhaktamsnati panchamam

The literal translation of this verse is: 'Sri Rama does not take meat or honey. He partakes every day of wild fruits and boiled (wild) rice fully sanctioned (for an ascetic) in the evening.'

Should I use Ayurvedic or Allopathic medicine?

Srila Prabhupada himself was once asked this question. He replied, 'Whatever works.'

Can I keep pets?

Devotees of Krishna are very kind to animals and we like them. But it has become a common practice now to bring animals indoors for our pleasure. This is not always helpful for the animals, as they belong in more natural surroundings. If we become emotionally involved with our pets, imagining that they experience human emotions or have become family members, that level of emotional projection becomes unhelpful. Animals living indoors can hardly keep themselves clean—it is often observed that the owner has to become involved in cleaning their mess. If one worships

Krishna inside the home, a pet can be unhelpful at cooking times or at times of meditation.

What's the harm in cricket, football or the so-called 'frivolous sports'?

It depends on whether you're playing or simply sitting and watching! One will keep you healthy and the other can get you over-excited or make you gain weight. In moderation, any game can help you as part of your physical exercise programme. But as in all things, too much sport can dominate your life and lead to the diminishing of spiritual activity. Over-consumption of sport simply as a fan won't help you physically or spiritually either. Again, it all boils down to what you consider your life's priorities.

Can you kill mosquitoes? What about rats?

It is best to not do it, especially if you don't need to. In India, the bites of mosquitoes can be avoided by protecting yourself with some insect repellent, specifically on exposed feet and elbows and at sunset or in dark areas. Rats arrive when there is food for them to eat, so cleanliness and placing all foods under cover are essential in dealing with them. As in other cases, prevention is much better than the cure (of killing). However, we do have permission to kill poisonous creatures, such as snakes and scorpions if they are a threat to health or life.

What do you do with holy pictures, sacred items or broken statues?

They should never be thrown away as rubbish. Traditionally, they are respectfully placed in a flowing river. But since the materials they're made of may, in modern times, not be environmentally friendly, and access to running water may be limited, a slightly better alternative is to dig a deep hole and bury them periodically.

Why do we have cremations instead of burials?

For some, burial is based on the conception that the physical body's resurrection will occur at the second coming of Jesus Christ. At that time, all the dead bodies will be revived intact from their graves. For others, burial is chosen due to the wish to preserve the body in death as in life. In the Vedic understanding, the body is a temporary vehicle for the eternal soul. Burning the body allows the soul to break its connection with all the false identities invested in that body so that it can move on to another destination. In the UK, cremations used to be the choice for only 20 per cent of all families of all faiths, now it is 70 per cent. One reason is that it is clean, relatively inexpensive and saves precious land space.

Do you practise yoga?

The word yoga actually means 'to join', like the English word 'yoke', when one thing is harnessed with another. The traditional process of yoga involves eight stages, the third and fourth of which involve physical postures and breath control. The postures (asanas) and the breathing (pranayama) make the mind peaceful for contemplation and meditation, the next stages. You may not see the devotees of Krishna in the temple do anything more complicated than sitting cross-legged, but it's enough for them to focus their minds on the sound of their mantra. Outside the temple, there are many devotees who practise and teach the postures of yoga.

Is there anything wrong with sex?

Sex is compared to a river—it's very useful but needs to be directed and retained by strong banks. When a river bursts its banks, it becomes a flood and can no longer be used in the same way. It can even be harmful. Sex within boundaries serves a purpose, but gratuitous sex can be personally and socially harmful. That's why every human society has some form of restriction.

Krishna orders that sex be regulated by the institution of marriage and for procreation.

If spiritual people are supposed to be detaching themselves from all things material, why do they get married and have children? Surely, that involves a certain amount of attachment.

Although life is very short from the point of view of the philosopher, the experience for most of us is that life is indeed very long, and in it, many challenges must be faced. Spiritual life is progressive, but that doesn't mean that there are no ups and downs. For the long race, it is generally advised that emotional stability is a great help.

The natural attractions of the world include the desire for a life partner, and the time-tested way of creating a long-lasting relationship is through marriage. Children are the natural consequence of marriage, and the next generation can be helped greatly when those children are trained in the art of Krishna consciousness. The world is overpopulated by people who care little, if at all, for spiritual life, and we need spiritual leaders to help heal the world. The purification provided by marriage, and the children produced, can help the individuals and the world greatly.

Why is sex within marriage supposed to be restricted? It's not illicit, so why is it not recommended for couples to have sex unless it's for procreation?

Sex is natural for the body—it's one of the important functions it was designed for by God. But the body and soul are different, and what is good for the body is not always good for the soul. In fact, the pleasures available to the body often serve to hinder the experience of one's real, higher identity. And that means that there is an ongoing struggle between one's self-realization and the lower urges. As you say, sex within marriage is not illicit, but by regulating the passions, we can make great strides upward in spiritual life. It may be regarded as a restriction by some, but for others, it will be an embracing of freedom.

Of course, it is something that is meant to be voluntarily accepted, and in a relationship, one's partner has to be in agreement. But many couples have experienced a rejuvenation in their marriage when, together, they have dedicated themselves to new goals in their relationship.

Are all the cultural items—clothing, language, food—necessary to practise Krishna consciousness?

Krishna consciousness is based on the principle of 'simple living, high thinking', where the cultural aspects are an integral part of the complete lifestyle.

Any form of dress that is decent, any language that can be understood and any food that is clean, pure and healthy, and can be offered to the Lord—all these can be used to practise Krishna consciousness. The dhoti, sari and so on can be produced very simply by handlooms, thereby making such clothing easily sustainable for generations living close to the land.

Food that is produced locally without unnecessary expense for transport is the best. Whilst devotion to Krishna is an internal adjustment that can be done by anyone anywhere, it thrives in and is safeguarded by a social culture that is land-based, environmentally aware and of good morals.

Why do you worship cows?

We don't worship anyone or anything apart from Krishna. But if something or someone is connected to Krishna, that becomes worthy of our reverence. Cows are essential to the life of humans, and we always respect them. They are considered sacred because they give us milk while the bulls plough the land from which grains come. Once a year, we give both special honours in the form of a short ceremony where they are publicly offered a lamp and some jaggery, or cane-sugar lumps.

Why all the fuss about the cow's poo?

We don't fuss, but *gobar*, or cow dung, is great for manure, excellent for fuel when dried, and, strangely enough, even considered to have antiseptic properties! If you keep cows, there's an unending supply of these helpful resources. Cow urine is even recommended by Ayurveda as a medicine.

Why do you eat with your right hand?

Everyone in the world eats either with a knife and fork, chopsticks or with their fingers. Eating with your fingers is considered helpful for appetite and digestion because you touch the food before you put it in your mouth. Because most people are right-handed, they use that hand for eating. There is a consequent practice of using the left hand for unclean tasks, which is helpful for hygiene too.

19

Holy Days and Festivals

There are places in the world that are sacred: holy mountains, rivers and forests. But there are holy calendar dates too. Sacred times mean celebrations and festivals. This section looks at some of the questions surrounding the holy days and festivals that are spread throughout the year.

Do you have a holy day, like Saturday for Jews or Sunday for Christians?

Every day is a holy day for a devotee, but devotees around the world tend to get together weekly according to when the working week of that country allows them. So in Muslim countries, devotees gather on a Friday, in Israel, they have Saturday feasts, and in many Christian countries, they have large gatherings on Sundays. Sometimes a mid-week evening is chosen because the weekends are set aside for visiting relatives and families with younger children. There is a special day every two weeks though, and on that day, we do extra things to remind us of Krishna.

What is that day called?

That day is called Ekadasi, which means 'the eleventh'. As mentioned earlier, it is the eleventh day after the full moon and eleven days after the new moon. On that day, the devotees do not eat any grains, beans or legumes, and try to chant extra names of Krishna and read more about Him. Some members even fast from all food on that day, but most honour the day by eating only foods free from wheat, corn, rice and so on.

You seem to celebrate a lot of festivals!

There is a lot to celebrate! In fact, every day there is an incarnation, the birthday of a saint or some other special event to celebrate. Of course, we have to choose only a limited number for our bigger public occasions, but our devotees celebrate in their way at home with their families.

What are your largest public festivals?

First in the year—February–March time—is the birthday of Sri Chaitanya Mahaprabhu, the golden incarnation of Krishna, who came to teach the process of self-realization in the current age, i.e. the congregational chanting of the names of God. Although He was Krishna, He had the colouring and compassionate mood of Krishna's most confidential devotee, Srimati Radharani. Devotees of the Hare Krishna movement are all followers of Chaitanya. He appeared in this world at the same time as the spring festival of Holi, the day when people throw coloured powders at each other in celebration of the new season. At this time, the story of Prahlada being saved from fire by Holika is also marked by burning a bonfire.

What's the next festival?

In April comes Rama Navami. The word *navami* means 'the ninth day' and on this day, many thousands of years ago, Lord Rama was born in the ancient capital of the Koshala province, the city of Ayodhya. Lord Rama and His young queen, Sita, His brother Laxman and faithful monkey-warrior Hanuman, are very well known throughout India. Their story has been told countless times in drama, dance and song. He appeared at midday, so devotees normally skip breakfast on that day and eat in the afternoon.

What about May? That is always a good time of year for festivals.

Yes, around that time, we celebrate the advent of the half-man, half-lion avatar of Vishnu known as Narasimha. He appeared to protect His young devotee Prahlada and in doing so, vanquished the demon Hiranyakashipu. The festival includes bathing the *archa-murti* of Narasimha with many liquids such as milk, yoghurt, fruit juices, honey and herbal waters. This festival is celebrated grandly throughout India and now all over the world.

Then comes Janmashtami?

Correct. This is by far the biggest festival of the year, during August–September. At Bhaktivedanta Manor near London, it is the biggest Krishna celebration outside India. More than 60,000 pilgrims come over two days. The festival celebrates the day when Lord Krishna appeared in the world. Krishna is, of course, always within the world, but this was the time when He became visible to all, and remained in the world for more than 100 years. Because He was born at midnight, the devotees fast all day, only eating after the celebration of the Lord's birth. Two weeks after Janmashtami, we celebrate another important festival, the birth of the Lord's eternal consort, Srimati Radharani. This festival is also on the eighth day, or *ashtami*, and hence is known as Radhashtami.

If it's a celebration, why don't you eat anything?

Fasting is a mark of respect for the divine person you are remembering. Eating tends to make you think of yourself! Although it's difficult at first, fasting does help you spiritually. And the time you save by not eating can be spent in some kind of spiritual activity. Fasting until midnight is perhaps the hardest fast of the year, but those who do it can testify to its spiritual power, especially by the middle of the night!

Do you also celebrate Diwali by fasting?

No! That's a day for feasting. For most Hindus, Diwali is the biggest annual festive period; a day for worship of Lakshmi and for honouring the gods one regularly worships throughout the year. For the devotees, it is the day when Lord Rama returns to Ayodhya after living in forest exile for fourteen years, battling with the evil king Ravana and being reunited with Sita. The inhabitants of the city lit lamps for Him as He came home, something devotees do in their homes to this day.

What about Dussehra?

That is two weeks before Diwali. It is also known as *Rama Vijayadashami* or 'the victory of Rama on the tenth day'. The tenth day of the moon of that month is when Rama defeated Ravana. In northern India, it is known as Dussehra, and on this day, a huge effigy of a ten-headed Ravana is burned and fireworks are set off.

It seems unkind to keep burning an effigy of someone who died thousands of years ago. Why don't you just drop that celebration?

It seems to be a popular festival that no one wants to drop. Certainly, the children would complain. Besides, the English are still burning Guy Fawkes who died in 1605! This particular festival highlights the ultimate destruction of evil after a long period of struggle—something that is analogous to our own struggle against our lower instincts.

What about Raksha Bandhan?

That is a popular custom celebrated by many in their families. We don't specifically observe it within the temple though. It also happens to come on the same day as the birth of Balarama, Lord Krishna's brother. So we tend to focus on that in particular.

What is Kartik? Is it a festival?

The entire lunar month of Kartik falls in October–November. The month is considered a special opportunity to perform devotional activity since it is said the results of any devotion are magnified in that period. One common activity that everyone can participate in is the offering of lamps in the temple. Offering a lamp is a sign of veneration, of offering something of value—heat and light—and of asking, through this small gesture, that one's devotion to the Lord will be increased.

Our particular focus during that month is the time when naughty child Krishna—during the Diwali period—was once tied to a wooden grinding mortar by His distraught mother, Yashoda. The vision of God Himself consenting to be restricted by His own devotee, out of His love, is said to be one of the most inspirational aspects of the affection between God and His devotees. So we sing about that and offer lamps to the Lord in that form. In that particular form, the Lord is known as Damodara, and so devotees also use the expression, 'the month of Damodara,' to refer to the Kartik month.

Why are the same festivals celebrated on different days by different groups?

India has different calendars in different parts of the country. In olden times, there was no way and no need to harmonize the different calendars. Celebrations took place according to local custom. These days, although the business world has universally adopted the Western Gregorian calendar, the calendars for religious observances still retain their regional differences. These are lunar calendars, which means the phases of the moon are used to mark the date. One calendar marks the beginning of the month the day after the full moon, and another calculates from the 'dark moon', the night when there is no moon in the sky. So, in different parts of India, some dates can even be two weeks apart.

The observance of specific events occurs according to the calculation of a particular 'lunar day' known as a *tithi*. A tithi is the duration of time it takes for the longitudinal angle between the moon and the sun to increase by 12 degrees. It does not have a fixed duration and can begin at varying times of the day. They range between nineteen and twenty-six hours in duration. As a result of this, certain solar days do not sufficiently overlap with tithis and are therefore not suitable for fasting or observing events. In such circumstances, the relevant observation is held the following day. Since a particular tithi occurs at different times in the world, a festival held in India on Tuesday might be celebrated elsewhere on Wednesday.

Finally, because the festival calendar is lunar, each month runs for one complete lunar cycle. That's twenty-eight days, which means the year of 365 days contains thirteen months. The Western calendar has months of twenty-eight, thirty and thirty-one days, (and sometimes twenty-nine), which means that the two calendars hardly ever match up. That's why these movable festival dates are generally given as February–March or October–November.

Are there any other festivals?

In southern India, many devotees like to celebrate Naraka Chaturdasi, a Diwali-time occasion marking Lord Krishna and Queen Satyabhama's defeat of the demon Naraka. There are many others, of course. Each temple has its local celebrations, but those are the large public ones. But I must tell you about one more—every year, three enormous, colourful wooden vehicles bearing the temple deities of Krishna, Balarama, and Their sister Subhadra are pulled through the streets. It is a grand, joyful spectacle and many thousands turn up to take part. It's called the Rathayatra. The word *ratha* means 'chariot' and *yatra* means 'journey'. It marks the long journey of Lord Krishna from Dwaraka to Kurukshetra, where He was reunited with His beloved friends from Vrindavan.

The culture of Sanatana Dharma has now spread all over the world, and this beautiful festival can now be found in London, where the parade concludes in a huge gathering in Trafalgar Square, the very heart of the city. In Los Angeles, California, the chariots are drawn in procession along the famous Venice Beach, near Hollywood, and in New York, down the city's most important street, Fifth Avenue. In Durban, South Africa, the festival continues for one week with many thousands attending, and of course, in India, there are many such festivals in cities throughout the nation—Kolkata, Delhi, Mumbai, Ahmedabad and Bengaluru being the prominent ones. Rathayatra now takes place in 100 cities worldwide. All these festivals are modelled on the original, which is still the biggest, attracting over 1 million worshippers. It has been held for centuries in the eastern seaside town of Puri, Odisha.

Do you celebrate Christmas or any other religious festivals?

Of course. Christmas, Hanukkah, Kwanzaa, Saint Lucy's Day and so on are winter festivals honoured by members of their respective communities, and many other religious and cultural festivals are celebrated throughout the year by people of different faiths and countries. We don't particularly celebrate Christmas at the temple, but no uplifting or religious festival is ever condemned. Our devotees come from many different communities, and we leave it up to them to choose which additional festivals or events they celebrate.

What is a yatra?

The word means 'movement' and is most commonly used to signify a religious pilgrimage, particularly to India. It's not a festival, but a sacred journey to live for some time in those holy places where Lord Krishna or Chaitanya Mahaprabhu descended into this world, travelled or performed some heroic deed. Devotees visit holy places like Vrindavan in Uttar Pradesh, Dwaraka in Gujarat, Jagannatha Puri in Odisha and Mayapur in West Bengal. Holy places in southern India such as Tirupati, Ahobilam, Kanchi, Rameshvaram, Srirangam, Thiruvattaru and Udipi are also popular. Devotees typically go to these places for 2–3 weeks and take advantage of a knowledgeable guide to show them around. There is also the more rugged option of *padayatra*, which means 'movement on foot', and refers to a holy walk. One popular such walk is the 128-mile, month-long barefoot pilgrimage around the land of Vraja, where child Krishna performed His heroic deeds. Because it is a circular walk for religious purposes, it is also known as a *parikrama*.

20

Guru and Disciple

One of the most important steps one takes in their path of devotion is that of accepting a spiritual master or guru. It is said that accepting a guru means you have made a commitment to spiritual practice and surrendered to accepting instructions from someone who you consider a representative of Krishna. You don't have to be around the devotee community very long before you hear the word guru. Not long after that, someone asks you: 'Are you initiated?' There's an entire study course for the subject of guru and disciple, but here are a few of the most common questions just to get you started.

What is a guru?

A guru is a teacher. Anyone who knows a subject and can teach it can be a guru. In India, there are gurus of music, pottery, archery, medicine and every other skill or department of knowledge. However, the word is most commonly used to indicate a person who teaches the most important form of knowledge—the science of self-realization. The Upanishads state that such a person will know the Veda, practise the teachings of the Veda in life and be 'firmly situated in transcendence'. A guru is also someone who has the compassion, ability and desire to teach others, has also been a faithful student of a guru, and whose teachings can be demonstrated to have brought about inspiration and transformation in the lives of others.

How do I know who is a guru?

When Lord Krishna told His friend Arjuna to approach a guru, He also told him the qualities of such a person. Thirty-six years later, when Krishna was about to leave the world, His friend Uddhava asked Him about finding a guru. Krishna advised him to find a *sadhu*, a 'good person', and gave him a list of twenty-eight qualities to look for in such a person. But the most important quality, said Krishna, was that the sadhu should be 'surrendered to me'.*

---

* Srimad Bhagavatam, Canto 11, Chapter 11, verses 29–32.

When Arjuna in the Bhagavad Gita asked Krishna twice about the qualifications of a truly self-realized person, the Lord told him that such a person gives up all selfish desires (2.55) and lives free from yearning, fear, passion and anger (2.56). If he has knowledge, he retracts his limbs from sense objects just like a tortoise (2.58), and he has genuine experience of something higher (2.59). Krishna also gave an extensive list of characteristics of someone situated in spiritual knowledge (13.8–12). The second time Arjuna asked, Krishna replied that a liberated soul is free from dualities such as joy and sorrow, praise and blame, honour and dishonour (14.22–25) and that one who serves the Lord with bhakti attains the Absolute (14.26). He also described the divine qualities that become manifest in a spiritually advanced person (16.1–3). Finally, the Lord asked Arjuna to abandon all other dharma and to surrender to Him alone (18.66), indicating that surrendering to Him is the sign of a fully liberated soul.

How can you revere human beings as gurus?

Gurus are revered because they give us the most powerful thing—knowledge. The Vedas are the best form of knowledge because understanding them can put an end to the problems of life, and a guru is one who has learned the Vedas, lives the Vedas, experiences their spiritual benefit and teaches them to others. Krishna is the original and ultimate guru who dwells within our hearts, but we often have difficulty listening to Him, so He kindly appears before our physical senses as a human representative. The guru is therefore not God, but the dear servant and messenger of God. As such, he is deserving of our reverence, respect, gratitude and service.

A police officer may be a mere human being but is obeyed because he represents the law; similarly, a guru is a mere human being—and always thinks of himself as such—but is revered because of who he represents.

What are the steps to finding a guru?

The first step is to study the life and teachings of Srila Prabhupada to learn how a self-realized soul behaves and speaks, what he teaches and how he guides. He is our example of a world-acharya, who all other devotees of Krishna, the sadhus, will need to be compared to. The second step is to write a list of the specific qualities of a sadhu to know what characteristics you're looking for. The third step is to find a sadhu who inspires you, who is able to encourage you and who can discuss your progress with you. The fourth is to check that the sadhu comes from an authorized lineage and that he was a faithful disciple of his guru. The fifth step is to confirm if he is accepting any disciples. The sixth step is to get ready to become a disciple.

Can women be gurus?

Since a sadhu is a person whose spiritual qualities shine through, and a guru is a sadhu who consents to teach others as disciples, the role of a guru is purely spiritual and neither male nor female. Both men and women have served in this capacity throughout history. But acting as a spiritual guide and teacher of sacred scripture, and acting as an exemplar of the tradition, are the most important features of a guru.

What is initiation?

Initiation means the beginning of something, and in Bhakti yoga, the word is used to indicate the formal beginning of the relationship between the guru and disciple. The Sanskrit word 'diksha' is also commonly used. At the time of initiation, the disciple makes formal vows to recite his mantra a certain number of times daily, to follow any rules and regulations the guru gives him, to study the Vedas, and to serve Krishna according to his ability. In return, the guru gives the disciple a new name, usually the name of God or a great saint. The name ends in the word *das* or *dasi* meaning 'servant'.

What does a disciple have to do?

A disciple is a student of a guru. He learns the scriptures from him, follows his example and moulds his life according to the guidance of the guru. A disciple makes a commitment to follow the disciplines of the spiritual path, to be determined in the face of life's challenges and to assist the guru in his service to his own spiritual master.

What offerings or gifts should be given to a guru?

That depends upon whether he is your guru or the guru of someone else! Traditional gifts are given to one's guru on completion of your education from him, or a tributary offering is made each year towards his maintenance. That may include grains, ghee, shoes, clothing or some other contribution towards living costs. The idea is to make a voluntary contribution—the guru is not supposed to ask for a specific amount. The best offering to a guru is to learn from him, follow his example, become perfected in the life he taught you and help others along the path.

Scan QR code to access the
Penguin Random House India website